The Legacy of

and

A Jewish Perspective

by Sheldon L. Lebold

Berwick Court Publishing
Chicago, IL

Berwick Court Publishing Company
Chicago, Illinois
http://www.berwickcourt.com

Lebold, Sheldon L.
  The legacy of Moses and Akhenaten : a Jewish perspective / by Sheldon L. Lebold.

  p. : ill., maps ; cm.

  Includes bibliographical references and index.
  ISBN: 978-0-9889540-1-4

  1. Moses (Biblical leader) 2. Akhenaton, King of Egypt. 3. Bible.--O.T.--History of Biblical events. 4. Jews--History--To 1200 B.C. 5. Egypt--History--Eighteenth dynasty, ca. 1570-1320 B.C. I. Title.

DT87.4 .L43 2013
932.014/092   *2013932980*

Dedication

This work is dedicated to my wife, Ronda, who has given me insight through the years and has provided to me the following important rule of interpretation:

Once is an incident;
Twice is a coincidence; and
Three times is a pattern.

As you read this work, any disbelief which may be experienced should be tempered by reflecting on the above rule of analysis and interpretation. I suggest that there are too many patterns in evidence to be the result of only a coincidence.

To see Sheldon's wife's striking resemblance to Neferti-ti, visit http://**bit.ly/LOMAronda** or scan the QR code with your mobile device.

CONTENTS

INTRODUCTION

Many people have opined that more wars have been based upon, or caused by belief in, religion than any other source. They have then concluded that religion is a source of evil, rather than being a force for good. I do not believe that that conclusion need apply to any religion; however, I submit that it does not apply to institutionalized Judaism.

The reader should note that this work is written from a Jewish perspective. But that does not mean that non-Jews should not read this work. I do not seek to proselytize; further, I do not denigrate other religions. I write little by way of comparative religious analysis of other monotheistic religions. In fact, it is obvious that, because Christianity has 2 billion followers and Islam has 1.5 billion followers, they are highly successful religions. Both Christianity and Islam very successfully provide hope to their adherents. However, Judaism has its own unique niche in the pantheon of religions.

I will not present any original research. Rather, I have analyzed existing sources and, I hope, synthesized same into a coherent text. Many others have treated some or all of the subject matter of this work, including: in antiquity, Manetho and Josephus; before World War II, Sigmund Freud; in more current times, Ahmed Osman and, additionally, Charles Pope and Moustafa Gadalla, who have expanded on Osman.

Independently, and on a separate, but partially related subject, Richard Elliott Friedman, author of *Who Wrote the Bible?*, has been a source of great enlightenment. His work relates to identification of the writers of the Torah. (The meaning of the term "Torah" is explained below, but generally refers to the first part of the Old Testament.)

A basic premise of this book is identification of the Pharaoh Akhenaten as Moses. For much of this text I refer to Moses/Akhenaten or, depending on the context, to Akhenaten/Moses. There is no difference intended in making such identifications of this person; the distinctions are merely emphasizing, in a literary manner, the primary identification of this individual at different points within the text. For purposes of this work, the followers of Moses and Aaron are called Hebrews, rather than Jews or Israelites. The Torah uses the word Hebrew until the Exodus from Egypt and not thereafter. However, in order to avoid any implication that the usage of different terms would have some subtle meaning, the term Hebrews is used, generally, throughout this book.

In making the above identification, I have found Osman to be greatly enlightening. I strongly recommend his books; in particular, I recommend *Moses and Akhenaten: The Secret History of Egypt at the Time of the Exodus*. My work does not seek to replicate his research and conclusions. In fact, I believe, whether read before or after this work, reading *Moses and Akhenaten* is an imperative. My goal has been, in part, to ground this book strongly enough in the text of the Torah and in the text of *Moses and Akhenaten* to provide a basis for the reader to follow the themes of this book.

Each of the aforesaid writers — Manetho, Josephus, Freud, Osman, Pope and Friedman — has had his own purpose or agenda. Osman and Pope deal, in part, with relationships between Moses and Judaism on the one hand and the life of Christ and the rise of Christianity on the other hand. Gadalla, in *Historical Deception: The Untold Story of Ancient Egypt*, has a similar treatment to that of Osman and Pope; however, his book further deals with the structure and workings of the ancient Egyptian civilization. Because the purposes and agenda of Osman, Pope and Gadalla are different from mine, their writings reflect a different treatment and emphasis.

But I have my own purpose and agenda. I have been amazed, in perusing the Internet, at the number of entries made on Jewish subjects by non-Jewish writers. Almost invariably, the greatest number of comments are those of Christians, Messianic Jews, Muslims, non-believers, black nationalist writers and outright anti-Semites. The Jewish entries are generally much fewer in number and much less intensive in content. Many of the Jewish writers merely recite and repeat the text of the Torah and/or the Talmud without any analysis of the text or reference to historical settings. This work has been motivated by an effort to give a more detailed and intensive review and analysis of subject matter from a Jewish viewpoint. In any event, I will try to identify, directly or by endnote, my reliance on the works of others.

Beyond dealing with historical events, my goal has been to address the role of Moses/Akhenaten in defining and establishing the Jewish people as an ethnic unit and, further, in creating Judaism as a force for good for both Jews and non-Jews. In this regard, it has often been said that Judaism acts as the conscience of mankind; I will review the meaning of that concept and how that concept evolved.

The core of my book is Chapter Seven, "Substance of a New Religion." It was the hardest chapter to write. It is the only chapter written in outline form, for ease of organization.

However, history is not two-dimensional. The various threads of the historical narrative interweave with one another. Examination of history is much like looking into a kaleidoscope: As one turns the kaleidoscope, the representation which one views changes and, as one continues to turn, continues to change. Similarly, some of the themes of this work are interwoven, because they have significance in more than one context.

There are those who will claim that this work is, effectively, a denial of the existence of God. That is not correct; in fact, such denial is not the thrust of this work. Just as evolution exists side by side with divine belief, a rational explanation of events and a rational explanation of personages exists side by side with divine belief. A friend of mine who has struggled with the question of the existence of God recently said that, in light of the Holocaust and similar painful human experiences, he still believes in a divine power, but he no longer believes in a "personal" God. From my own perspective, dealing with historical facts and events does not bring an end to theology and divine belief but, rather, provides a new beginning for study and understanding. Belief in God is a matter of faith; faith exists, or co-exists, with historical facts.

I must also deal with issues presented by religious arguments from many that the Bible, whether Old or New Testament, is the "Word of God." I can accept the concept of divine inspiration, but reject the concept of immutability. In fact, ordinary reading, as well as intensive textual analysis, readily discloses inconsistencies and historical contradictions in the holy books. Textual analysis discloses that there were earlier texts to which reference is made in the Torah which have not survived to this date. For example, there were the Book of Yashar, the Book of the Battles of Yahweh and the Chronicles of the Kings of Judea; those texts would have amplified our understanding of the Torah text. Furthermore, as noted, there is no single interpretation of the texts. Rabbis have debated the text and meaning of the Torah for thousands of years.

By way of illustration, numerical expressions in the Torah as to time (years), and as to numbers of people, animals, or things, are often less than accurate. For example, to indicate that a personage was 900 years old may be acceptable as a matter of faith, but as a matter of biology it is impossible. Therefore, I have attempted throughout this book to make comprehensible, and realistic, certain dates and certain population numbers.

Despite these difficulties, these texts (and for our purposes, the Torah) continue to speak to us. The better we understand the origins and meaning of the text, the better we can apply its messages to our own lives.

I cannot claim that everything that I have written, and the conclusions which I have reached, are fully correct. But I will be satisfied if I achieve one of two results as a consequence of my efforts. First, my work may result in a better understanding and appreciation of the Jewish historical record and thereby give insight as to the scope and power of what Moses/Akhenaten and the Levites accomplished. Second, I hope that it will provide to others a springboard for further and fuller analysis of the subject matter from a Jewish perspective, so that Jewish learning will be reinvigorated and curiosity will be, become and remain an active part of one's "Jewishness."

ﬡ

PARABLE

Here is a story. At the end, you may be able to identify the person who is the subject of the story.

A baby boy of Hebrew descent is born in an area of ancient Egypt identified as Goshen. The area is inhabited by numbers of Hebrews and, at least for part of the year, by members of pharaonic royalty. Members of the Egyptian priesthood lobby the pharaoh for the death of the boy. However, by intercession of female members of the Egyptian royal family, the boy survives and is raised as a member of the royal family. He learns to speak Egyptian as his first language. He learns and lives the royal customs and practices. He is raised as a prince within the household of the ruling royal family. He has a significant and meaningful relationship with his older sister, who is approximately 5 to 7 years older than he. As he grows into young manhood, our man of royalty turns from a belief in the traditional gods of Egypt to a belief in a single God. He develops and refines his beliefs into full-scale monotheism, a belief in a universal and singular God.

An incident occurs wherein one or more Egyptians is killed and wherein our royal subject favors a Hebrew involved in the homicide. Our royal subject feels concern for his own safety and, as a result, withdraws from the royal palace and escapes to hide in the Sinai. He lives there in exile for many years. When he later becomes aware that all those who sought to kill him are dead, he returns to the royal palace and place of residency of the newest claimant of the pharaonic seat. He takes with him his rod or staff, bearing a serpent's head, which is an imperial sign of Egyptian royalty. He is accompanied by a Levite compatriot. There is a confrontation at the imperial court between our royal subject and the new pharaoh and, while the new pharaoh generally rebuffs the petitions of our royal subject, the pharaoh gives him the right to lead a mixed multitude, comprising the Hebrews of Goshen, the Levites and others, past the outposts of the Egyptian empire into the Sinai. An Exodus occurs, the pharaoh changes his mind about safe passage, the Egyptian army pursues and the Egyptian army is duped into making a deadly mistake, which leads to its defeat and destruction.

Who is our hero?

Most Jews, Christians and Muslims would identify our hero as Moses. However, Egyptologists or archaeologists might well identify him as the Pharaoh Akhenaten (Amenhotep IV).

The biographical information of our story fits both Moses and Akhenaten because, as others have demonstrated, they were effectively the same person. As to Moses/Akhenaten, this work deals with three goals: First, with the proof of that identification; second, with an examination of the beginning of the Exodus; and, third, with examination of the growth and development of Judaism as a result of the life and philosophies of Moses/Akhenaten and of interaction of Moses/Akhenaten with the Levite priesthood.

2

CONUNDRUM

Here is a question: What circumstances in Egypt gave fertility to the activities and religious innovations of Moses/Akhenaten?

In answer, let us note that the religious beliefs of the Egyptians prior to Moses/Akhenaten were largely polytheistic in nature, although the preeminent god at that time was Amun. The religious rites and practices were largely driven by a desire of the royalty and the wealthy citizens to achieve immortality. A manifestation of these rites and practices was mummification of the deceased. The process of mummification was very costly. These rites, practices and costs gave rise to a large and entrenched hierarchy of priests. To say the least, this priesthood was very powerful.

As we will see, Moses/Akhenaten challenged and disempowered this priesthood. He not only established monotheism, but also installed his own priesthood, the Levites, and erected his own temples. He moved the seat of government and religion to his own capital city and religious center, Akhetaten. These actions ultimately resulted in violent confrontations. A description of this power struggle is given by Ahmed Osman, as follows:

> It was … the loyalty of the army, controlled by Aye, [Akhenaten's uncle], that kept Akhenaten in power in the uneasy years that followed his coming to the throne as sole ruler in his Year 12 upon the death of his father. By that time Akhenaten had developed his monotheistic ideas to a great extent. If

the Aten was the only God, Akhenaten, as his sole son and prophet, could not allow other gods to be worshiped at the same time in his dominion. As a response to his rejection by the Amun priests as a legitimate ruler, he had already snubbed Amun and abolished his [Amun's] name from the walls and inscriptions of temples and tombs. Now he took his ideas to their logical conclusion by abolishing worship of any gods throughout Egypt except the Aten. During the Amarna rule of Akhenaten his subjects were totally committed by the king to the worship of a monotheistic God, although at this time only the Levites among the Hebrews were involved in his new religion. Akhenaten closed all the temples, except those of Aten, dispersed the priests and gave orders that the names of other deities should be expunged from monuments and temple inscriptions throughout the country. Units were despatched [sic] to excise the names of the ancient gods wherever they were found written or engraved, a course that can only have created mounting new opposition to his already rejected authority.[1]

The Egyptian records reflect the foregoing societal upheaval. Do other records corroborate this conflict? Yes, as we will note throughout this book, the Torah and Talmud do.

Most members of Western civilization are aware of the Bible. For Jews, the Bible generally means the Old Testament. The Old Testament comprises:

A. The five books of Moses (also known as the Torah)

B. The Prophets

C. The Writings

The aggregate of these components is called the Tanakh. Unless otherwise indicated, we will be dealing largely with the Torah.

The Talmud comprises the oral traditions, which have been reduced to writing. The Talmud commences with the Mishnah. The Mishnah is then expanded by the first of the commentaries, being the Gemorah. Both the Mishnah and Gemorah are then further subject to commentaries by other writers. The aggregate of the written compendium of text, starting with the Mishnah, is called the Talmud.

The Torah is historical, but not in a modern sense of a historical treatise. It is a compendium of many diverse things, including folklore, religious matters, covenants, laws, priestly concerns, morality, psychology, poetry, prose, military strategy and history. For Jews, it is a political text, partly in the nature of a Declaration of Independence and a Jewish Constitution.

It is also polemical. The Torah is replete with references to, descriptions of and judgmental evaluations concerning the society, political structure and social and religious mores of ancient Egypt. While, as will become readily apparent, there was in fact a symbiotic relationship between the Hebrews and the ancient Egyptians, the Torah deliberately does not identify by name the several pharaohs to whom reference is repeatedly and sequentially made.

These polemics were not an accident. By the time of reduction of the Torah to writing, the several authors of the Torah were attempting to promulgate their respective *Jewish* points of view. They collectively wanted to separate their views of Judaism from one another and also from actual Egyptian history. So they deliberately blurred the identity of the historical participants and historical events. The proof of such obfuscation is shown by comparing the lives of Joseph and of Moses. The Torah provides a magnificently personal exposition of the interaction of Joseph with his brothers upon their reunions. There is deep psychological interplay. Therefore, a reader cannot say that the writers of the Torah did not understand the technique of writing intensely personal stories. They did. In comparison, however, there is almost nothing nearly as descriptive or intensely personal concerning Moses. One of the objectives of this text is to create, as much as possible, a biographical study, which is both historical and psychological, of Moses.

Conversely, but in a parallel manner, the pharaohs who reigned subsequently to Akhenaten, as well as their priests and military officials, wanted to eradicate the records of: 1) the existence of Akhenaten; 2) monotheism as the Egyptian state religion of the Amarna[a] period; and 3) the social, religious and military upheaval caused by, during and after the reign of Akhenaten. They took great pains to physically eradicate and re-write the records and monuments of the Amarna period. So, the records of the Egyptians and of the Torah do *not* dovetail. But clues as to what happened, as historical fact, are replete within the Torah, Talmud and Egyptian sources.

It is commonplace for many commentators to critique the Torah and the history of Egypt. Some even deny the existence of Moses and of the Exodus. These critiques come from both Jewish writers and non-Jewish commentators. For example, the noted editor H. H. Ben-Sasson, in the very extensive treatise entitled *A History of the Jewish People*, writes of the "complete silence of extra-biblical sources on the descent of the children of Israel into Egypt, their residence in the land of Goshen and the subsequent Exodus to Canaan." Again and further: "The absence of any extra-biblical sources for the Exodus and Conquest of Canaan can be accounted for, in all likelihood, by the fact that these events carried insufficient international weight to be recorded in contemporary accounts."[2]

Dr. J. H. Hertz, editor of one of the main Torah and Haftorah commentaries, also recognizes deficiencies in analyzing the history of the Exodus and the actions and motivations of Moses. He refers to Akhenaten as Ikhnaton in four different places of his text; however, he summarily rejects viewpoints other than strict interpretation of the text. He is very dismissive in his commentary.

I think the opposite of these commentators. I believe that the reign of Akhenaten and his activities as Moses were, from an Egyptian viewpoint, histori-

---

a   The cultural, artistic, architectural and literary period Akhenaten created during his reign is called the "Amarna" period.

5

cally cataclysmic in nature. That reign and those activities continued over a period of time of approximately fifty to eighty years, resulted in joint Hebrew-Egyptian suppression of the record of the period and of these events and, further, resulted in mutual historical revisionism.

Some of the impetus for the Egyptian revisionism was due to a natural event. As I will later explain, Amenhotep III, the father of Akhenaten, created a co-regency with his son in order to ensure Akhenaten's legitimacy as the next pharaoh. During that co-regency and into the beginning of Akhenaten's reign as the sole pharaoh, Egypt was gripped by an intense plague. As Pope notes: "The plague of that time is known from archaeology to have ravaged the entire Near East, and it struck Egypt especially hard."[3] Recovering from its destruction was the main preoccupation of the final four pharaohs of the Eighteenth Dynasty. Pope further expands:

> Akhenaten's religious reforms may have succeeded had they not coincided with a terrible plague that was spreading throughout the entire Middle East. … When the plague did not relent, the thousands of unemployed priests and servants of Amun's Temples had all the more reason to blame Akhenaten's reforms and his rejection of the God who had brought Egypt so much prosperity in the past.[4]

Pope concludes: "The strife associated with the Exodus, and which ultimately brought down the Egyptian 18th Dynasty, was largely an overblown family feud during a time of intense adversity and suffering."[5]

The cataclysmic nature of this fifty- to eighty-year period was civil unrest that almost resulted in civil war. Osman graphically portrays the picture of religious conflict between supporters of the god Amun and supporters of the god Aten and, further, portrays societal unrest in this manner:

> The persecution of first Amun and then the other gods, which must have been exceedingly hateful to the majority of the Egyptians, would certainly also be hateful to the individual members of the army. This persecution, which entailed the closing of the temples, the despatch [sic] of artisans who entered everywhere to hack out his name from inscriptions, the presumed banishment of the clergy, the excommunication of his [Amun's] very name, could not have been carried out without the army's active support. Granting the fact that the theoretical fiction of the divine kingship was accepted by the mass of the Egyptian people, it is, nevertheless, hardly credible that they would just sit by and acquiesce silently to the persecution of Amun. Some strong backing had to support the royal dicta. Each time a squad of workmen entered a temple or tomb to destroy the name of Amun, it must have been supported by a squad of soldiers who came to see that the royal decree was carried out without opposition. Ultimately, the harshness of the persecution must have had a certain reaction even upon the soldiers who, themselves, certainly had been raised in the old beliefs.[6]

This picture of friction may have resulted in military battles and may have given rise to the complaint of Queen Tiye, Akhenaten's mother (as is more fully described in Chapter Seven), that "surely a bridegroom of blood are thou [Akhenaten/Moses] to me" (Exodus 4:25).

Richard Elliott Friedman is brilliant in his review and analysis of the text of the Torah and of part of the additional books of the Tanakh. He and other authors have named five writers of the Torah. Friedman identifies them as being: J, E, P, D and the Redactor. He further suggests their motivations in writing their versions. J relates to the writer who identifies the divine name as Yahweh/YHWH/Jehovah; the J stories fit the territory of the historical southern kingdom of Judah. The J stories look upon the life and activity of Aaron in a most favorable light; the writer was probably a descendant of Aaron. The author of J may have been a female.[7] The J stories are more concerned with women and are much more sensitive to women than are the E stories. The E stories are associated with the divine name Elohim; the E stories fit the territory of the historical northern kingdom of Israel. The E stories present Moses in a most favorable light; the writer was probably a descendant of Moses. The author of E was a male. P is attributed to the priests and is probably a work of the Aaronid priesthood in the age of King Hezekiah. P interweaves stories and establishes law codes. The author of P was also a male. The D stories present both law codes and also the farewell speech of Moses before his death. The D stories are contained in the Book of Deuteronomy. The D stories are separated into two "editions." The first edition ends with the reign of King Josiah. Friedman identifies the writer of the second edition as Baruch, son of Neriyah. Finally, the fifth writer is the one who combined all five of the books and is called the Redactor. Friedman identifies the Redactor as Ezra the Priest, or as he is sometimes designated, Ezra the Scribe. Friedman, in his analysis, gives insight into the historical development of the text of the Torah and into the motivations of the five principal writers for writing as they did.

No doubt additional efforts will continue to unlock the "secrets" of the Torah. Similarly, Christians and Muslims also have their own interpretations of the text and stories of the Old Testament, and of their respective sacred books.

By way of illustration, comparison should be made of the list and content of the Ten Commandments. First, there are two statements of the Ten Commandments. They are in Exodus 20:2-14 and, later, Deuteronomy 5:6-18. The words of each of these two recitations of the Ten Commandments are not identical in the Torah. Further, the numbering of the Ten Commandments by different religious denominations is not necessarily identical. As to content, there are substantive differences. For example, the prohibition against homicide in the Hebrew text is "Thou shall not *murder*." For some, but not all, Christian denominations, that prohibition changes to "Thou shall not *kill*." As to the New Testament, the writers, such as the writers of the Four Gospels, are often identified by name. The codification of the four Gospels is exclusive of the many other Gospels that were written but were not included in the Canon. In any event, the contributions of each of the writers of the four Gospels are not necessarily internally consistent with the contributions of the writers of the other Gospels. The text of The Book of Revelations presents, by itself, a huge enigma which invites analysis.

So, having examined the historical and textual background, let us proceed to examine the historical ancestors and antecedents of Moses/Akhenaten.

3

JOSEPH AND YUYA

Proof of the identity of Moses/Akhenaten starts with identifying biblical Joseph and verifying his existence.

The Torah tells the story of Jacob having two wives, Leah and Rebecca. Jacob has a total of eleven children with Leah and two concubines; these are ten sons and one daughter. He also has two children with his favorite wife, Rebecca. These children are Joseph and Benjamin. The Torah and Talmud tell the story of resentment among the sons of Leah and the two concubines toward Joseph. The children of Leah and the two concubines see Joseph as being the favorite son. Joseph receives a coat of many colors from his father, which only serves to increase the resentment of the brothers. The brothers then sell Joseph into slavery. He ends up in Egypt. The brothers soil the coat of many colors with goat blood to prove to their father, Jacob, that Joseph has been killed.

Once in Egypt, Joseph has a number of encounters and adventures and, ultimately, interprets a dream to the pharaoh in power. Osman identifies that pharaoh as Tuthmosis IV. Tuthmosis IV reigned for a short period of time, but during that period he appointed Joseph as vizier (prime minister). Tuthmosis IV was succeeded by his son, Amenhotep III, who continued to retain Joseph as an adviser or prime minister.

Osman also provides persuasive identification of biblical Joseph as an Egyptian dignitary named Yuya.[1] He provides pictures of the mummies of Yuya and

Tuya, his wife. He points out non-Egyptian features, consistent with Semitic origin, of the eyes, chin and nose of the mummy of Yuya. Yuya has a beard, which is a Semitic, not an Egyptian, characteristic, because the Egyptians were clean shaven. His ears are not pierced, unlike the ears of most royal mummies of that time. His hands are placed in a manner, which, while not pharaonic, indicates a deceased person of great reverence. The sarcophagus of Yuya contains a necklace similar to, or the same as, the one to which reference is made in the Torah.[b] There is, finally, DNA and other conclusive evidence in the tomb that tie Yuya to his great-grandson, Tutankhamun, the son of, and successor to, Akhenaten.

More dramatically, the funerary artifacts contained in the tomb of Yuya describe Yuya as being "Holy father of the Lord of the two lands."[2] The Torah quotes Joseph as saying: "[God] hath made me a father to Pharaoh and lord of all his house and ruler over all the land of Egypt."[3] Before further analyzing the foregoing, it is necessary to observe that the Torah sentence has two parts. The first part is: "[God] hath made me a *father to* Pharaoh" (emphasis added). Hertz indicates that the phrase "father to" is without great significance and is simply reflective of an Egyptian title of state rank. I disagree. If the subject phrase were insignificant, it could have been left out. In this regard, we should compare the foregoing phrasing with the wording of Genesis 41:41, which states: "And Pharaoh said unto Joseph: 'See, I have *set thee* over all the land of Egypt'" (emphasis added). Further, compare the foregoing phrase with Genesis 42:6 which states that "Joseph was the *governor* over the land" (emphasis added) or with Genesis 45:9: "God hath made me lord of all Egypt." If the phrase "father to pharaoh" were eliminated from Genesis 45:8, the meaning of the balance of the sentence would remain unimpaired and would correlate with the quotations from 42:6 and 45:9. Therefore, it would appear that inclusion of the phrase had some significance to the writer of the text. Osman states that the term "father to pharaoh" means, literally, that Yuya was the biological father, or forbearer, of one or more pharaohs. Because of the foregoing identification (including, dramatically, the DNA sample results), the phrase "father to," as used in the Torah text by Joseph in conversing with his brothers, appears to be a literal acknowledgement *by Joseph* that some of his descendants were pharaohs. The first of those pharaonic descendants was Akhenaten/Moses, Yuya's grandson. The second was Tutankhamun, Yuya's great grandson. The third was Aye, Yuya's son, who, despite his age at the time of his coronation, became a pharaoh shortly after the death of Tutankhamun.

We will now return to the second part of Joseph's sentence. In parsing the terms, we should note that the Hebrew term for Egypt is in the plural: Mitzraim. This plural term reflects the Egyptian description of its territory as comprising both Upper Egypt and Lower Egypt. So, as one compares the foregoing phrase and sentence, one notes a distinct parallelism:

---

b   Photographic evidence of Yuya's necklace can be seen in Osman's *Hebrew Pharaohs of Egypt,* included in photographic insert between pages 54 & 55 of book 1.

> **Holy Father**   *of the Lord*
> He hath made me *father* to Pharaoh and *lord* of all
> ***of the two lands***
> his house and ruler over all the *land of Egypt*.

The parallelism is striking, but the Hebrew text has been expanded deliberately to avoid ascribing divinity to pharaoh through usage of the Egyptian term "lord." The term "lord" in the Hebrew text has been used in the sense of overlord or land manager, rather than as used in the Egyptian wording in the sense of supreme ruler [god] of the land of Egypt.

Further, as Osman and Pope point out, the first syllable of Yuya's name is a common Hebrew reference to, and diminutive form of, YHWH. That diminutive form is "YU," or "JO"; it is used in the names of Joash, Joel, Jochanan (John), Jonathan, Joshua and Josiah. The female name, Jocheved (referred to in the Torah as being the mother of Moses), also contains the diminutive form of YHWH.

When Tuthmosis IV appointed biblical Joseph to be, effectively, his prime minister, he designated him with an Egyptian name, "Zaphnath Paaneah."[4] It appears that strangers, generally, as well as Joseph, specifically, were given Egyptian names when brought into positions of importance for, and acting on behalf of, the royalty. By compounding and joining the first syllables of both the Hebrew and Egyptian names, one obtains:

1. **Yu**ya[5]   Yu..........
2. **Zaph**nath Paaneah[6]   ......Zaph
3. Yuzaph
4. Yuseph (Joseph)

Interestingly, the tombs of Yuya and Tuya, his wife, were situated next to that of Tutankhamun. Since Tutankhamun died substantially after Yuya and Tuya, and since his tomb could have been placed anywhere, it is apparent that his tomb was *deliberately* situated adjacent to the tomb of his great-grandparents, Yuya and Tuya. Other than an early break-in to the tomb of Yuya and Tuya, their tombs and Tutankhamun's were some of the only known tombs to have survived antiquity in a relatively intact condition.

The body of non-royal Yuya had been embalmed (mummified) and placed in a sarcophagus; this fact parallels the last verse of Genesis in the Torah (50:26), which states, regarding Joseph: "They embalmed him, and he was put in a coffin in Egypt." The next to last line of Genesis (50:25) is: "And Joseph took an oath of the children of Israel, saying: 'God will surely remember you, and ye shall carry up my bones from hence.'" Osman suggests that this sentence was a later addition to the original text.[7] He makes reference to Donald B. Redford, with whom he usually does not agree, but reports that Redford similarly reached the conclusion that the second to the last sentence was a later addition. Friedman points out that the J stories do not make any reference to a deathbed request by Joseph that his bones should be carried back to Canaan for burial;[8] this request is only made in an E story and apparently results from an attempt by the author of E to elevate the importance of the (northern) kingdom of Israel.

There are many other relationships between Yuya and Joseph. For example, there was a gold chain found in Yuya's sarcophagus; in Genesis 41 the text is that the pharaoh "put a gold chain about [Joseph's] neck."[c]

Also, Osman points out: "Chariots have played an important part in the debate about when exactly Joseph lived in Egypt. They are mentioned three times in the biblical narration. The first is when Pharaoh appointed Joseph as his vizier: 'And he made him ride in the second chariot which he had; and they cried before him, Bow the knee: and he made him ruler over all the land of Egypt.' (Genesis 41:43)"[9]

As to the above verse, Osman states that the "second chariot … suggests his [Joseph's] responsibility for the chariotry."[10] The suggestion is that, subject to the primacy of the pharaoh, Joseph was placed in charge of the chariotry and charioteers.

Again when Jacob arrived in Goshen with his family: "And Joseph made ready his chariot and went up to meet Israel his father, to Goshen." (Genesis 46:29)

This verse indicates ready access to a military vehicle by a person of importance and high rank. Also significant, as Osman notes, is the inclusion of chariots in Genesis 50:7-9: "And Joseph went up to bury his father. And with him went up all the servants of Pharaoh, the elders of his house, and all the elders of the land of Egypt. And all the house of Joseph, and his brethren, and his father's house: only their little ones, and their flocks, and their herds, they left in the land of Goshen. And there went up with him both chariots and horsemen."

Hertz comments on this verse that: First, the reference to "the elders of the land of Egypt … [shows that] the respect shown to Jacob is evidently due to the great position occupied by Joseph in Egypt." He further suggests that the reference to chariots and horsemen signifies use of a military guard to protect the procession. This reflects a military cohort led by Joseph as a military commander.[11]

With respect to the foregoing, Osman quotes Alan Richard Shulman, the American philologist, as concluding that:

> However, in the later Eighteenth Dynasty two ranks are attested which indicate that such a technical nuance has come into being: [First,] adjutant of the Chariotry … the earliest occurrence of which is known from the Amarna period (of Yuya, who was appointed as Adjutant Deputy of His Majesty in the Chariotry as well as Officer for the Horses), and [second,] The Standard-Bearer of the Chariot-Warrior. It would thus seem that by this reign (Amenhotep III) chariotry was thought of as a separate entity, and we may

c Genesis 41:42 also states that pharaoh took off his signet ring and put it upon Joseph's hand. This ring was never found in the coffin; this is understandable because, in ancient times, thieves had broken into the tomb. The ring was apparently a target for the thieves' attention.

assume that the army had been reorganized into the two arms of infantry and chariotry, each with its own organic and administrative components, at about that time.[12]

Osman concludes: "Thus the first person in Egypt to be appointed to the position ascribed to Joseph in the Bible was Yuya."[d]

It is noteworthy that the relics found in Yuya's tomb included "a chariot, in perfect condition, which was at that time only the second chariot known to have survived from ancient Egypt."[13] This relic indicates the importance of chariotry in the life of Yuya.

Osman suggests that the three Torah references referred to above support a conclusion of identifying Joseph (of the Torah) with Yuya, who bore a royal title (among other titles) of Master of the Horse.

We can also further correlate the Torah with the Egyptian records. The Torah states that Joseph had two sons. The Egyptian records show that Yuya had two sons *and a daughter*. This is not a contradiction because, as Osman points out, females were often omitted (or reduced in stature) in the text. Yuya's daughter was (Queen) Tiye, who became the Great Royal Wife of Amenhotep III, father of Akhenaten. She is a key to further analysis and identification of the last four pharaohs of the Eighteenth Dynasty.

Further, the Torah states in three places that the descent of Hebrews into Egypt was comprised of seventy persons.[14] Sixty-nine of them, all men, are identified by name. The unnamed seventieth person would have been Queen Tiye.[15]

Finally, we should address the issue of the number of pharaohs under which Yuya/Joseph served. Osman adduces proof that Yuya served two pharaohs. First, he was appointed as vizier by Tuthmosis IV; second, he served as vizier for Amenhotep III. The Torah does not deal with the issues of the numbers of pharaohs under which Joseph served. But the Talmud does:

> And it came to pass ... that Pharaoh the friend of Joseph died. ... Before his death, Pharaoh commanded his son who succeeded him, to obey Joseph in all things, and the same instructions he left in writing. This pleased the people of Egypt, for they loved Joseph and trusted implicitly in him. Thus while this Pharaoh reigned over Egypt the country was governed by Joseph's advice and counsel."[16]

Identification of the mummy of Yuya as being the mummy of Joseph proves the existence of Joseph as a real person, as opposed to positing that Joseph was merely a creation of folklore or an allegorical creation of a biblical writer. Without that verification, we are left in a position of being unable to pursue our historical detective work, because there is no "starting point." In such case, we could not refute the argument of those who deny the existence of Moses, deny the circum-

---

d   While many other scholars suggest that chariots were introduced to the military in earlier Hyksos times, Osman argues that this is just an assumption; he states that the military aspect of the chariots was introduced and established by Yuya.

stances relating to the Exodus and deny that the Exodus ever occurred. However, with that verification, we can now pursue, as a matter of fact, the existence and identification of Moses/Akhenaten. We can further establish and fix the identity and relationships of many of the personages and events of the Torah. Again, there are too many inter-connections to be dismissed as incidents or coincidences. There are definite patterns.

4

MOSES AND AKHENATEN

As suggested in Chapter One, Moses/Akhenaten flees to the desert. He stays there for about 25 years. Then, at the urging of God and upon advice that all those who sought to kill him were dead (Exodus 4:19), he returns to the seat of government to regain his throne or, alternatively, to seek freedom for his Hebrew co-religionists. While the Torah states that all Jewish male babies in Egypt were to be killed, the Talmud suggests that only Moses specifically was to be killed. Osman states:

> The Talmud story confirms that it was the survival of Moses that Pharaoh wanted to prevent, because, once he knew that Moses had been born and survived, his attempt to kill all the Israelite children at birth was abandoned: "After Moses was placed in the Nile, they [Pharaoh's astrologers] told Pharaoh that the redeemer had already been cast into the water, whereupon Pharaoh rescinded his decree that the male children should be put to death."[1]

Pharaoh Amenhotep III was of royal blood. He designated Queen Tiye as his Great Royal Wife. While Queen Tiye was the daughter of Yuya and Tuya, she was not of royal blood. Amenhotep III and Queen Tiye had two sons, Prince Tuthmosis and Amenhotep IV — also known as Akhenaten. (For ease of further reference, we will identify Amenhotep IV as Akhenaten even though he assumed the name Akhenaten only at a later time in his life.)

Prince Tuthmosis had mysteriously died prior to the birth of Akhenaten, being perhaps murdered by the Amunite priests. Because Akhenaten was, like his brother, of Hebrew descent, the priests of Amun pressured Amenhotep III to kill, or permit them to kill, his second son, Akhenaten.

The priests applied this pressure because they identified Hebrews with earlier Semitic intrusions into Egypt. The throne of Egypt had been co-opted by victorious Semitic incursions beginning approximately in 1659 BCE. Those Semitic incursions led to the Hyksos reign, which lasted approximately 108 years. The Hyksos people were considered to be shepherds and the Egyptians looked upon shepherds as an abomination. This negative evaluation of shepherds is reflected in the Torah in two places: 1) when Joseph has dinner with his brothers in the palace and tells his brother to misidentify their occupation (Genesis 43:32); and, again, 2) when Joseph tells his brothers to misidentify their occupation to pharaoh (Genesis 46:33-34).[2]

Queen Tiye saved her son's life by sending him at an early age to live with her Hebrew relatives in Goshen. While royalty was passed to males in a matriarchal manner (through the queens, rather than the kings), Amenhotep III had no further male descendants with Queen Tiye. Therefore, Amenhotep III, at the urging of Queen Tiye, protected Akhenaten against further machinations of the priests. Akhenaten was then acknowledged by Amenhotep III to be the sole and rightful heir. Later, to consolidate Akhenaten's rights to the throne, Queen Tiye convinced Amenhotep III to designate his son as a co-regent, thus creating a *fait accompli* as to kingship.

The co-regency between Amenhotep III and Akhenaten lasted for approximately twelve years, ending at the death of Amenhotep III. During that time, the rupture between the Amunite priests and Akhenaten had grown more acute. Queen Tiye convinced Akhenaten to move the capital from Thebes and build a new royal city. The move apparently occurred in the eighth year of the co-regency. The new royal city was called Akhetaten.

Before proceeding with the life of Moses/Akhenaten, we should consider the derivation of the name Moses. It is generally accepted that the name "Moses" is of Egyptian origin. As Friedman states: "It is among the Levites ... that we find people with Egyptian names. The Levite names Moses, Hophni and Phinehas are all Egyptian, not Hebrew."[3]

Osman expands on this by referring to the analysis of Sigmund Freud's last book, *Moses and Monotheism*: "Freud was first persuaded to take [the view that Moses was an Egyptian] by the fact that Moses was itself an Egyptian name. ... How ... can we expect the Egyptian royal mother to have sufficient knowledge of the Hebrew language to be able to choose a special Hebrew name for the child?"[4] Further, how can we expect the Egyptian royal mother to have a sufficient motivation for choosing a Hebrew rather than an Egyptian name for her royal son? Osman points out that the Egyptian name "Mos" means "child" and, more significantly, "rightful son and heir."

After Akhenaten fell from power, the Egyptian authorities forbade any verbalization of his proper name; violation of the prohibition was punishable by death.[5] Akhenaten was then officially referred to as "The Fallen One of Amarna." Osman postulates that the Hebrews called him "Mos" as a code name to indicate that, to the Hebrews, he was and remained the rightful heir to his father's throne. Osman points out that the second "s" at the end of the name Moses is drawn from the Greek translation of the Biblical name and not from the Egyptian or Hebrew languages.[6]

It should be noted that "Mos" was a common part of other Egyptian names, such as: Ptahmos, Ahmos, Tuthmos, Ramos and Kamos. It is further interesting that the Talmud ascribes no less than six other names to the baby Moses before the Torah definitively establishes his name as Moses. This reinforces the observation and suggestion of Freud and Osman that Moses is an appellation that was later supplied by a writer of the Torah.

It is similarly useful to consider other Hebrew/Egyptian names. For example, the name of the sister of Moses is, in the Torah, Miriam. This name ("Mry") is Egyptian and means "beloved." Meryet/Merit ("beloved") was the generic name in Egypt for the royal heiress.

Akhenaten's Great Royal Wife was his childhood sweetheart, Nefertiti. Miriam/Nefertiti was a half-sister of Moses/Akhenaten and was approximately 5 to 7 years older than he. The supposition exists that Akhenaten and Nefertiti were betrothed to each other at birth because Nefertiti was of royal blood. Because the monarchy passed by way of matriarchal descent, the marriage of Akhenaten to the royal princess Nefertiti would add to the authenticity and legitimacy of Akhenaten as the rightful heir to the throne.

While under current mores it is unacceptable and incestuous for marriage to be between brother and sister, such circumstances were acceptable in Egyptian royalty. Pope states that:

> It is difficult if not impossible for us to understand Akhenaten's family life, and the culture of that time. The account of Sophocles states that his marriage to his mother was not for love or pleasure, but was a "service to the state." Right or wrong, royalty reserved for themselves the exclusive right of human breeding for the purpose of establishing their superiority over commoners. We may as well just lose our self-righteous indignation. Who doesn't want some improvement in the genetic department?[7]

(Pope also makes a further connection between Akhenaten and the Greek stories of Oedipus.)

Hertz also acknowledges that: "In Egypt, marriage with a sister was quite usual, especially in royal families."[8] The Torah further specifically states, in Exodus 6:20, that Amram (identified as being the father of Moses) was married to his aunt (father's sister).

The primary priest of Akhenaten's religion, which for our purposes we shall call Atenism, was Meryre II. This name has the same Egyptian root as Miriam. There were, in fact, two Meryre personages related to the priesthood of Atenism. Meryre II, from the same name-root of "Mry," relates to Aaron. This same name-root is used repeatedly in the Torah to describe one of the tribal elements of the Hebrews during the Exodus: the "Merari."[e] The priests of Atenism were apparently descendants of the tribe of Levi. The Levites were, historically, descendants of the patriarch Jacob. They served as the priesthood of and for Akhenaten in his state religion. After the fall of Akhenaten from the imperial crown, they were the primary supporters of Moses in the exile in Sinai.

It is appropriate at this point to consider who the Levites were and how they became the priests of Atenism. Based on the chronology set forth in Appendix II, the Hebrews, including the Levites, as a large group of people, lived in Egypt for only a few (approximately four) generations. It is not credible to believe that the Levites could have developed sophisticated priestly practices in such a short period of time. The question is, therefore: How could they have become the priests of Aten and, after the Exodus, of the Hebrews? In answer to that question, we should note that the second of Yuya/Joseph's sons was Anen. Anen was a high priest, being the Second Priest of Amun in Thebes. He died in approximately year 30 or 34 of the reign of Amenhotep III, which was shortly after creation of the the co-regency between Amenhotep III and Akhenaten. When Anen died, his priestly followers would have been superseded by priests of the new high priest, Simut.[9] As earlier noted, Akhenaten by that time had been rejected by the Amunite priesthood. In response, Akhenaten had turned the tables and rejected the Amunite priests. He began to build his own capital and religious center at Ahketaten. He needed a priesthood to serve in his new temples. Anen's priests would then have constituted a perfect group to serve as the priests of Aten. It is likely that they, together with the Levites who believed in a monotheistic religion similar to Atenism, joined to form the new priesthood. With input by Moses/Akhenaten, they would have created new priestly practices and functions which, with little change from the practices and pageantry of the Amunite priesthood, would have comprised, almost immediately, a fully functioning Atenite and, thereafter, Hebrew priesthood of monotheism.

In any event, the Levitical priests lived in a city west of the Nile and across the river from the royal city of Akhetaten, created by Akhenaten as the seat of his religion and of his royal palace; the municipality of the Levites was called Malevi, meaning "city of the Levites." The name Aaron means, in the Egyptian language, "mountain of strength" or "light bringer." The chief servitor of the religion of

---

e   It is perhaps significant that the Merari were situated in the configuration of the camp next to the "Sons of Aaron," *closer* than were the non-Levite tribes. Hertz actually creates a map of this configuration.

Atenism was "Panhesy"; Panhesy corresponds to the name Phineas who was a descendant of Levi and was designated (Numbers 25:10) to be the source of the continuing line of High Priests.

The name-root of "Mry" applies, as noted above, to Miriam, Meryre II and Merari. While the root of the word means "beloved," and while, with respect to Miriam/Nefertiti, that was the generic name in Egypt for "royal heiress," it might be more illustrative to compare the name of "Mry" (beloved) to the expression: Your Royal Highness. When one addresses the Queen of England, one would not say "Queen Elizabeth," but rather "Your Royal Highness."

The Torah skips the childhood of Moses. In Exodus 2:10-15, the text is: "And the child grew. … And it came to pass in those days when Moses was grown up … he saw an Egyptian hitting a Hebrew. … And he looked this way and that way and when he saw that there was no man, he smote the Egyptian. … Now when Pharaoh heard this thing, he sought to slay Moses. But Moses fled from the face of Pharaoh and dwelled in the land of Midian."

In a few short sentences, we proceed from the birth of Moses to his exile in Sinai. By itself, this story makes no sense. If a high-ranking member of the Egyptian royal family killed someone, why would the pharaoh not just accept the incident as a prerogative of royal power or, alternatively, as justifiable homicide because the royal personage was merely protecting royal property? However, Osman provides an alternate possibility from Egyptian sources. He states that, found in the Amarna ruins, there was a letter sent to Akhenaten by Abd-Khiba, King of Jerusalem, in which the king accuses Akhenaten of allowing the Hebrews to kill two Egyptian officials without being punished for their crime. Moses/Akhenaten was warned by his uncle, Aye (who became a later pharaoh), of a plot against his life, whereupon Moses/Akhenaten abdicated and fled to Sinai, taking with him his pharaonic symbol of authority, the rod or staff topped by a bronze serpent. Osman continues:

> One can even see the character of Aye as the man who, according to the Koran, advised the king to leave the city as the chiefs (nobles) were plotting to kill him.
>
> > And there came a man,
> >
> > Running, from the furthest end
> >
> > Of the City. He said:
> >
> > "O Moses! the Chiefs
> >
> > Are taking counsel together
> >
> > About thee to slay thee:
> >
> > So get thee away, for I
> >
> > Do give thee sincere advice." (Sura XXVII, 20)[10]

This story has a parallel in the Talmud:

19

When Moses fled from Egypt he joined the army of Kikanus, [the King of Ethiopia] and soon became a great favourite with the king and with all his companions.

And Kikanus became sick and died…

So the army appointed Moses to be their king and leader…

And the Ethiopians placed Moses upon their throne and set the crown of state upon his head, and they gave him the widow of Kikanus for a wife. …

During this time Moses was reigning in Ethiopia in justice and righteousness. But the queen of Ethiopia, Adonith … said to the people, "Why should this stranger continue to rule over you? Would it not be more just to place the son of Kikanus upon his father's throne, for he is one of you?" …

Moses voluntarily resigned the power which they had given him, and departed from their land. The people of Ethiopia made him many rich presents, and dismissed him with great honours.[11]

Osman points out that "the name of the Queen who became the wife of Moses is given as Adonith (Aten-it) and that name is clearly derived from the Aten, the one god whom Akhenaten attempted to force upon the Egyptian people." In the course of analysis, Osman suggests that Adonith is a code name for Queen Tiye.[12] (The quotation regarding gifts of rich presents will become relevant in a later discussion of the Exodus in Chapter Six.)

As noted, the Torah skips the childhood of Moses. But quickly, in Exodus 4:2, the text refers to a "rod" held by Moses. One of the signs of imperial authority of a pharaoh was a scepter in the shape of a serpent either made of, or covered with, brass. The Passover Haggadah parallels this fact; it refers to the phrase, "And with signs." According to *Haggadah of the Sages*: "that [means] the rod (of Moses) as it is said: 'and you shall take this rod in your hand, with which you shall do signs' (Exodus 4:17). The connection between the expression 'and with signs' and the [Torah] verse is clear. … There is a great deal written about Moses' rod and its role in the Exodus."[13]

It is interesting that the Torah, in Numbers 21:6-9, attempts to establish the reason for existence of the "snake set upon a pole." The text is: "And the Lord said unto Moses: 'Make thee a fiery serpent, and set it upon a pole …' and Moses made a serpent of brass, and set it upon the pole." This text seems largely unrelated to the surrounding texts in that chapter.

Hertz comments about this text and suggests that "this brazen serpent made by Moses was naturally preserved as an object of veneration by the Israelites. But when in the course of centuries it tended to become, and eventually became, an object of idolatress worship, it was destroyed by King Hezekiah."[14]

I disagree with Hertz. There are three reference points in the Torah and Tanakh pertaining to the scepter. First, there are references in Exodus, such as in 4:2

and 4:20. We will call these the initial references. Second, the text of Numbers 21:6-9 sets forth a relationship between snakes and punishment of rebellious Hebrews. We will call this the middle reference. Third, there is a reference in the Second Book of Kings referring to the destruction of the staff of Moses. We will call this the final reference.

I think that the passage in the middle reference has no purpose, other than to provide a convenient reference point for a writer of the Torah text to connect the final reference to the middle reference. If one deletes the middle reference, it becomes clear that the final reference relates back to the initial references in Exodus, which describe the confrontation of Moses/Akhenaten with Pharaoh Ramses I, where the staff had significance as a sign of Egyptian imperial authority. I submit that the middle reference in Numbers was likely a later insertion that was used as a means and method for the writer of the Torah text to deliberately hide the connection of Moses/Akhenaten to his pharaonic past.

King Hezekiah could have *avoided* veneration of the scepter by requiring it to be hidden from view and held with other objects in the bowels of the Temple Mount, or in another non-public place or storeroom. His action in smashing the imperial staff was a result of his desire to eliminate, from the Jewish religious history of the Exodus and of Moses, the existing proof and symbolism of the Hebrew connection to Egyptian royalty.

There are other religious parallels between Moses and Akhenaten, but those will be pursued later, in Chapters Six and Seven.

5

CHRONOLOGIES, GENERATIONS AND THE PHARAOH OF OPPRESSION

We can now correlate the relevant pharaohs of the Eighteenth Dynasty and their years of reign with corresponding Hebrew generations and their approximate dates of birth. These correlations are set forth in two tables which are included in Appendix II.

Reference to those two tables will, from time to time, provide a frame of reference and insight into the people and the historical timeline. So let us turn our attention to Aaron. The Torah identifies Aaron, in a strange way, as the brother of Moses. In Exodus 4:10-14, we are first introduced to Aaron as follows:

v 10 And Moses said unto the Lord … "I am not a man of words … for I am slow of speech and of a slow tongue."

v 13 And he said: "Oh Lord, [identify] him who thou will send."

v 14 and he [God] said: "Is there not Aaron thy brother the Levite? I know he can speak well."

Let us correlate Aaron's position to the family tree of the Eighteenth Dynasty. In Appendix II, we can begin our analysis by noting that Yuya/Joseph was the father of Queen Tiye, the wife of Pharaoh Amenhotep III, and also of Aye, the military supporter of Akhenaten. Aye was the husband of Tiy.[f] Aye and Tiy were parents of Mutnedjmet, the wife of Horemheb, who became Akhenaten's cousin through marriage. Osman expands on this situation by identifying Tiy, the wife of Aye, as the wet nurse of Miriam/Nefertiti and of Akhenaten/Moses. Tiy had given birth to her own child. Osman posits that this biological child was Aaron; he suggests that Aaron was, in fact, a "feeding brother" to Miriam/Nefertiti and Akhenaten/Moses. He points out that: "Even today, bedouin children ... nursed by a woman [will] call her 'mother,' the same name that they use for their real mother."[1] He further states that the Koran confirms that Moses and Aaron were related only through the feeding-mother relationship. When Moses came back from the Mount to find the Israelites worshiping a golden calf, he becomes very angry, so he:

> Seized his brother by (the hair
>
> Of) his head and dragged him
>
> to him. Aaron said
>
> "Son of my mother!" (Sura VII: 150)[2]

We are aware that, while Akhenaten was not himself truly a military man, he was surrounded and supported by the army in Akhetaten. He kept the throne through military power and might. Pope notes the following:

> A mural in the tomb of the Egyptian noblemen May depicts Tutankhamun and his "cabinet members." The six men who stand behind Tut in the mural include the four generals who would follow him on the throne. They are his uncle, Aye, Haremhab [sic], Ramses and Seti. All four of these generals ultimately turned against Akhenaten.[3]

Aye, like Akhenaten, was of Hebrew descent. Aye supported Akhenaten for as long as he could, perhaps because of one or more of the following: avuncular love; a possible promise made to Yuya that he, Aye, would protect Yuya's grandson; affinity with religious reform instituting monotheism as the state religion; or the desire to hold and maintain power.

Horemheb shared a family relationship with Akhenaten through his wife and father-in-law. Horemheb was not only a cousin through marriage of Akhenaten, but also, as noted, one of Tutankhamun's military generals. Nonetheless, Osman identifies Horemheb as the Pharaoh of Oppression. What explains the total reversal of Horemheb's relationship with his cousin-in-law, Akhenaten? It is imperative that we understand the answer to this question, so as to have a better ability to

---

f   There is a similarity of spelling between Queen Tiye and the wife Tiy. In Egyptian, the names may have been identical. However, as noted, Tiy and Queen Tiye were distinct and very separate individuals.

accept the validity of this identification.

There are several possible reasons for the reversal of the relationship between Horemheb and Akhenaten. First, Horemheb may have wanted raw power. Second, once he had achieved the status of King, Horemheb would have wanted to consolidate his power; in order to do this, he had to receive religious support. He could not rely on the Levites because they continued to support Atenism and, more importantly, because the Levites supported Akhenaten as being the high priest of Aten. He could not rely on the former priesthood of Amun because that priesthood had its own power base. Consequently, he created a new priesthood drawn from the military, which was under his control. This action would have required repression and suppression of all non-supporting religious ideologies. Third, he may have wanted to quell any civil unrest resulting from the turmoil created by, and resulting from, the religious reforms of Akhenaten, which were abhorrent to much of the Egyptian citizenry. Fourth, Horemheb may have perceived that Akhenaten had been so distracted with his religious obsessions that he had become ineffective as a leader. Horemheb may have believed that, to save the monarchy, a dictatorial regime and repressive measures were required. Fifth, he may have bridled under the rule of his cousin-in-law, believing that he himself was better suited to be the ruler. Sixth, he was not of Hebrew descent. For any or all of these reasons, the identification of Horemheb as the Pharaoh of Oppression is psychologically sound and believable. When the Torah states: "Now there arose a new king over Egypt, who knew not Joseph," (Exodus 1:8) the meaning is not that the Pharaoh of Oppression did not have knowledge of the existence of Joseph/Yuya. Rather, it means that he rejected Joseph/Yuya and all that he and his descendants represented. Horemheb might have seethed with resentment at any reference by his wife to her father, Aye, and her grandfather, Joseph/Yuya. After all, as noted, Horemheb was not of Hebrew descent.

Horemheb had one major failure. He left no descendants. His death ended the Eighteenth Dynasty. He effectively caused the establishment of the Nineteenth Dynasty, starting with his appointment of Ramses I as pharaoh. Ramses I was succeeded immediately by Seti I and then by Ramses II. As we will see, Ramses I and Seti I figure prominently in the Exodus.

6

EXODUS

I n examining the history of the Exodus, there are in fact two perspectives. One
is the familiar Hebrew version; the other is the Egyptian version. The entire
period which we will examine was short and, significantly, the common de-
nominator to this entire period is Moses/Akhenaten.

The Exodus is clearly a seminal event in Jewish history, but some aspects of
the story, which are left out or only alluded to, are crucial to our understanding
of the legacy of Moses/Akhenaten. In this chapter we will examine the history of
events and also the motivations of the participants from both sides. We will then
examine the mechanics (and engineering) of the actual escape from Egypt.

Reviewing the history and the royal figures should be simplified by referring
to Appendix II, which sets forth the names of the pharaohs and their respective
periods of rule.

The contrast between the Egyptian and Hebrew viewpoints is shown in the
following two quotations. First, a common Jewish explanation of the bondage and
enslavement of the Hebrews is set forth in the Passover Haggadah by Rabbi Martin Berkowitz, of Temple Adath Israel of the Main Line, Merion, Pennsylvania,
wherein he states:

> There were but seventy people who arrived in Egypt, but, in time, their
> number increased. Soon they grew also in strength and became a mighty
> people. The Egyptians came to fear them for, they reasoned, in time of war

27

they might join with enemy nations and become a threatening force. They, therefore, decided to subdue them with forced labor, and to reduce their numbers by casting male children into the river. Task masters were placed over the Hebrews, who whipped and tortured them, compelling them to make bricks and build great cities for Pharaoh.[1]

The Egyptian view of the history is reflected by Osman:

Amenhotep III became concerned about the growing power of the Israelites and sought advice about how to deal with them. But this cannot be simply because they had grown in number and might side with his enemies: the growth in their numbers would simply have provided him with more slaves to work for him and made him stronger in the face of foreign aggressors. What we are dealing with is a religious revolution. The vast increase in the numbers of the Israelites by this time was not simply a matter of their birth rate: the declaration by Moses that the Aten, his God, was the only true God, had attracted many Egyptian adherents who, as a result of their conversion to the new religion, became regarded as Israelites. Other evidence suggests that the Israelites had also achieved political importance and high position in the land, with, according to Manetho, priests and learned people in their ranks. At the same time, those of Moses' followers who did not follow him to Amarna were, according to Manetho, set to harsh work in the stone quarries.[2]

This comment of Osman is interesting, but Osman does not address the reason for the "attraction" to the new religion. It appears that the Amunite (and other polytheistic) forms of Egyptian religion appealed, and were directed, to a particular segment of Egyptian society, being the royalty and the wealthy who could afford mummification and the creation of monuments, which were designed to facilitate reincarnation. While there were apparently many festivals in which the common citizenry could participate, they certainly could not have afforded the costs of mummification. Also, as will be noted later, the Egyptian religion dealt with fatalistic and never-ending cycles of life and death. Contrariwise, Atenism and the Hebrew religion were tied to a more open and inviting effort of finding divinity in the progress and unfolding of history. While the Atenistic conception of God is abstract and, therefore, could be remote to some of the common citizenry, the ability of the common person to more personally identify with the God of the new religion may well have caused the attraction, suggested by Osman, of many Egyptian adherents to the new religion.

The seventeenth year of the reign of Akhenaten was effectively his last. Most scholars believe that Akhenaten died in that year. However, there is no evidence that, while he ceased ruling, Akhenaten then died. No mummy of Akhenaten/Moses has ever been found, further reflecting the lack of proof that Akhenaten/Moses had died at that point. If he had died or been assassinated, the most immediate and simplest treatment by the priests of Amun would likely have been acknowledgment of the death of Akhenaten/Moses with a grand funeral to ratify, through funerary observance, of the joinder of the old and new regimes, as in the phrase: "The King is dead, long live the King!"

Osman suggests that monarchical legitimacy was directly related to the land. (We note the significance of this idea and its transference into Jewish religious tradition in Chapter Seven.) Because a pharaoh gained power from the gods and, through the gods, sovereignty over the *land*, Akhenaten/Moses would not surrender his royal status to the priests or to any other group. Rather: "It is true that Aye and his army stopped him from exercising his power, but he was still regarded as the legitimate ruler." When Akhenaten/Moses then went into exile, the Amunite priesthood refused to accept Tutankhamun as his successor until Tutankhamun rejected the Aten. Once Tutankhamun accepted the concept of being the son of Amun (rather than being the son of Aten), which he did in year four of his reign, the Amunite priesthood accepted him as king and celebrated this new change with a coronation celebration. It was only then, when he no longer could claim a religious relationship to the *land*, that Akhenaten/Moses stopped being king.

As previously noted, during the reign of the Pharaoh of Oppression (Horemheb), verbalization of the name of Akhenaten was forbidden. Officially, Akhenaten was referred to by the Egyptians as the *Fallen* One of Amarna (rather than as the *Deceased* One of Amarna). It is most reasonable to assume that the Hebrews avoided the proscription against utterance of of the formal name "Akhenaten" by referring to him with a code name, as Moses (or Mos), which means "rightful heir."

The Hebrew view of history is reflected hereafter.

In the Torah, Moses flees to the desert, stays there for about twenty-five years, and returns at the direction of God to seek the release of the Hebrews from bondage. Evidence suggests that Akhenaten/Moses was about 35 years old when he went into exile in the Sinai. Therefore, when Akhenaten/Moses returns to seek release of the Hebrews, he was approximately 60 years old.[3]

When Moses/Akhenaten went into exile, he would have been accompanied by a coterie of supporters. There would have been military protection for three reasons: 1) There would have been a security detail, much in the nature of Secret Service protection of an ex-president of the United States of America; 2) some of the military would have been rejected in the regime of the next pharaoh, Tutankhamun, as they were tainted by having been supporters of Akhenaten/Moses; 3) some of them would have joined the exiles because they were true devotees of the new religion. The issue of safety is reminiscent of the circumstance which presented itself, after the end of the United States War of Independence, to former loyalists and supporters of the English crown. Because of their loyalist sympathies, they were looked on unsympathetically. Many of them moved to New Brunswick and Nova Scotia, Canada, or back to England, for their own comfort and safety.

There would have been Levites accompanying Moses/Akhenaten, because they were the priests of Aten (and Akhenaten was the proponent of their theology that the Aten was the single supreme being). In this regard, the Talmud acknowledges that the Levites, who did not reside in Goshen, were not enslaved.[4] Further, they had no position or function in the hierarchy of the Theban priests of Amun or, later, in the military priesthood appointed by Horemheb.

It is interesting to speculate that Moses/Akhenaten and his coterie of supporters would have probably disguised their facial appearances by growing beards and by otherwise taking the appearance of non-Egyptian residents of the Sinai. Such disguises would have effectively given them a modicum of protection, because they would not have then been readily identified as supporters of Moses/Akhenaten by passing Egyptians who were loyal to subsequent pharaohs. We will further consider the use of disguises in Chapter Nine.

Belief in the survival of Akhenaten/Moses is borne out when, approximately twenty-five years after Akhenaten/Moses left the throne, Horemheb died. The Torah relates that God called Moses and his Levite brother, Aaron, to return from exile because "all those persons who sought to kill him [Moses] were dead" (Exodus 4:19). These verses provide the first introduction in the Torah of Aaron and identify Aaron both as a Levite and as a brother to Moses. Moses claimed that he would have trouble communicating with the Hebrews of Goshen because he was poor of speech (Exodus 4:1-14). While there is a Talmud story relating that the speech and verbal skills of Moses were impaired when he burned his tongue as a child on a hot coal, the Torah verse initially only refers to communication with Hebrews in *their* language, but does not reflect any reluctance or inability of Moses to converse with the pharaoh in the Egyptian language. In other words, the difficulty of speech resulted from lack of familiarity with the language spoken by the Hebrews as contradistinguished from speaking in the Egyptian language, which was the language of Moses/Akhenaten as a member of Egyptian royalty. (Later, for internal Torah consistency, there is a Torah reference that Moses also had difficulty in speaking to the pharaoh; however, this difficulty is not emphasized and the further texts indicate no continuing difficulty in verbal expressions.)[5]

Moses/Akhenaten returns with his imperial rod or staff to regain the crown (because he was the last surviving member of the Eighteenth Dynasty), but his effort was rejected by the pharaonic designee of Horemheb, Ramses I, who wielded military power.

During the twenty-five year period of exile before the Exodus, Moses and his supporters would have explored the geography of the Sinai. They would have been required to find places to hide and places to live. They would have been required to develop routes of commerce to acquire foodstuffs and sundries. They would have developed routes to return (or to send people) to Egypt for exchange of information or to pursue lifestyle events, such as births, deaths and marriages. Moses/Akhenaten would have used such lines of information to become aware of the death of his son, Tutankhamun, the accession and conclusion of the reign of

Aye and the accession and death of Horemheb. Perhaps such lines of information are reflected in the verse: "Go, return into Egypt; for all the men are dead that sought thy life" (Exodus 4:19).

It is significant that, while the entire Sinai Peninsula, east of the north-south Samana Canal (the location of which we will discuss below) was considered to be in the nature of a protectorate of Egypt, it was not an integral part of the empire and was not occupied with a military garrison. Therefore, a dissident group could surreptitiously live in that area.

Osman posits that Moses/Akhenaten probably spent a substantial amount of time in a mountainous area in the southern portion of the Sinai Peninsula called Sarabit.[g] Sarabit has ruins which indicate that it was occupied over an extended period and that, at some time, it was occupied by members of Semitic tribes. There are remains of a number of pools for retention of water which apparently had been used for ritual washing. (This topic is further developed in Chapter Seven.)

Osman reports that fragments of a limestone stela made by Ramses I were found at Sarabit:

> What was surprising about the stela is that in its inscription, Ramses I describes himself as the "The ruler of all that the Aten embraces." Of this unexpected reappearance of the fallen Aten, Petrie comments: "To find the Aten mentioned thus after the ruthless Amunism of Horemheb is remarkable. Hitherto the latest mention of it was under King Aye."
>
> The name of the Aten had been missing for thirteen years during the reign of Horemheb; now at the time of his successor, Ramses I, the hated God has appeared, not in the Egypt proper but in Sinai. The stela made more than a quarter of a century after Akhenaten's fall from power, also features the Amarna realistic style. ... [Ramses I's figure at the top of the stela] is carefully wrought, and in the dress resembles the work of Akhenaten. ... This was not the only surprising discovery. At the temple [was] found the dark green head, executed in the Amarna style, of a statue of Queen Tiye, Akhenaten's mother.[6]

In contrast to Ramses I, Horemheb might have known of the presence of Hebrews in Sinai, but he may have not felt challenged because he was a "legitimate" member of the Eighteenth Dynasty. However, after the death of Horemheb, Ramses I was perhaps challenged to establish his paramount monarchical position by eliminating any vestiges of the Eighteenth Dynasty and "neutralizing" the community of Moses/Akhenaten. Alternatively, the purpose of building that stela might have been an effort by Ramses I to ingratiate himself with the resident Hebrew community of exiles for the purpose of dampening unrest among the exiles and avoiding (unsuccessfully) the incident now known as the Exodus. In any

---

g   While Hertz refers to the high places as being, effectively, Mount Sinai, such as in Exodus 3:12, that verse merely says a mountain. The discussion by Osman more convincingly identifies the mountain in Exodus 3:12 as being Sarabit.

event, the action by Ramses I, of "invading the space" of Moses/Akhenaten and his followers and installing the stela, may have been a pivotal action; it might be similar to a challenge to a dual wherein one party slaps the face of the other.

Prior to this challenge, Moses and his followers had spent their time in exile with efforts to create a sustainable community and a sustainable philosophy and theology. From the beginning of the exile through the date of death of Horemheb, Moses/Akhenaten had taken no action to regain the throne or to obtain the freedom of the remaining Hebrews in Goshen. But, once Pharaoh Ramses I had undertaken an offensive (in both the affirmative and repugnant senses of the word) action to undermine the authority of Moses/Akhenaten and the Levites in Sarabit, it is likely that Moses/Akhenaten and his followers felt they had to respond in order to defend and preserve both their community and their religious existence. The Sarabit community was aging and Moses/Akhenaten and his followers would have recognized that, upon the death of the leadership, the remaining resident community might have dissolved. Moses/Akhenaten and the Levites would likely have experienced growing recognition that "new blood" would be required to maintain the community. As a consequence, they apparently created a complex plan for, in the first instance, attempting to regain the throne or, in the second instance, maneuvering or tricking Ramses I to release the Hebrews of Goshen. If they were successful in effecting the release, Moses/Akhenaten and his followers would have at least acquired a pool of young followers for the new religious order. The final part of the plan of Moses/Akhenaten was to create a military strategy for drawing Ramses I and his charioteers out of an area of safety and into an area of military ambush.

I will skip the story of the ten plagues because, while they provide a background and precursor story to the story of the Exodus, they do not generally affect the flow of the Exodus event. There is one exception: Upon the end of the tenth plague, the Torah recites that the pharaoh relented and that Ramses I "called for Moses and Aaron by night, and said, 'Rise up, get you forth from among my people, both ye *and the children of Israel*" (Exodus 12:31, emphasis added).[h]

It would have been interesting to have been present at the confrontation between Ramses I and Moses/Akhenaten. One could conjure that the pharaoh would have shown surprise at the direct challenge to his authority by the appearance of Moses/Akhenaten. Ramses I would have been angry at the attempt by Moses/Akhenaten to prove, to the Amunite priesthood, that he, Moses/Akhenaten, was the legitimate ruler. In order to dismiss Moses/Akhenaten, Ramses I might have acceded to the request of Moses/Akhenaten to permit the Goshen workforce to leave Egypt; he would have been resigned to that economic loss, and relieved

---

h   Compare this to the later description in Exodus 12:38 of a "mixed multitude." This would appear to suggest that the initial Exodus was considered to be composed of Hebrews while, upon occurrence of the actual event, there were more people, and of more backgrounds, than just the Hebrews.

at the removal of the Hebrews in Goshen, who constituted, effectively, a "fifth column" which threatened to undermine his authority.

Conversely, one could conjure that Moses/Akhenaten had approached the pharaoh fearful that he and Aaron might be killed on the spot. Moses/Akhenaten would have been angered at the rejection by Ramses I of the superior claim of Moses/Akhenaten to assume, and recover, the throne. But he would have been relieved that Ramses I had agreed to the request to release the remaining Hebrews of Goshen. He would have been satisfied and, in fact, have had an appearance of slyness, at the success of maneuvering Ramses I into a position of imminent military retribution.

In any event, the tension between Moses/Akhenaten and Ramses I must have been great, because they were contemporaries and in great competition with each other from historical, political, religious and economic perspectives.

With respect to economics, there follows an interesting passage (Exodus 12:35-36): "and the children of Israel … asked of the Egyptians jewels of silver and jewels of gold. … The Egyptians … let them have what they asked and they *despoiled* the Egyptians"[7] (emphasis added). The Talmud, as previously noted with respect to the kingship of Moses/Akhenaten in Ethiopia, repeats that same theme of transfer of gold and assets. Finally, it is significant that the Torah states "the children of Israel went up *armed* out of the land of Egypt" (Exodus 13:18, emphasis added).

Before proceeding with the story of the Exodus, we should again note that, while Moses/Akhenaten was in exile, the reigns of Tutankhamun, Aye and Horemheb occurred. Pharaoh Aye reigned for only four years. His reign ended abruptly. With respect thereto, the Irish and Scots have folklore that the followers of Pharaoh Aye left Egypt upon the end of his reign. They took a large sum of gold and other treasures and, after a short stay in Iberia (Spain), they moved on and inhabited the "Isle of Destiny," being Ireland and Scotland. This story is perhaps supported by current Irish family surnames of "Aye," archeological findings in Ireland of tombs that were built in a manner consistent with Egyptian practices, finding of a mummified head embalmed in accordance with Egyptian methods, and, most importantly, unearthing of gold torcs (which were necklaces worn by Egyptian royalty).[i] Such a transfer and looting of gold, precious jewels and metals would have been less than popular with the next pharaoh, Horemheb, and with his royal ruling classes.[8]

Returning to the story of the Exodus, the Torah recites (Exodus 14:5) that "it was told to the King of Egypt that the people were fled." Most assuredly, the

---

i   When writing this book, I mentioned the subject matter to a close friend, Brian McGuire. His eyes lit. He said he knew all about that history. He then removed a gold ring from his finger and showed me the inscription on the inside of the band. It said: "Pharaoh Aye 1320 BC." While the date is slightly different from that set forth in Appendix II, the emotional impact on me was startling!

transfer and removal of wealth was also told to the king. The removal and looting of wealth by followers of Moses/Akhenaten would appear to have been a repetition of the earlier actions of the followers of Pharaoh Aye (as above noted). The action of the followers of Moses/Akhenaten, as reflected in the Torah and Talmud, would likely have resulted in a backlash, magnified by memory of the earlier incident of transfer and looting of wealth by the followers of Pharaoh Aye. As a result, the Pharaoh Ramses I reneged and gathered a war party to pursue the Hebrews.

The Torah specifically reflects the route taken by Moses in Exodus 13:17: "God led them not by the way of the land of the Philistines." The Hebrews were not to proceed on the coastal road, the road of Horus, on the north. Irrespective of other biblical explanations, it would have been too easy for pursuers to catch the escaping Hebrews on the road of Horus. That road was flat ground and provided a well-traveled or paved roadway. It would have provided no defensive position for the escaping Hebrews. But, in Exodus 13:17: "God led the people about [south] by the way of the wilderness of the Yam Suph; and the children of Israel went up and on the land of Egypt." As Moses/Akhenaten prepared to defend against a likely onslaught by the pursuing Egyptians, the Hebrews would have, as previously noted in the Torah (Exodus 14:2), backed against the Yam Suph, "and Pharaoh will say of the children of Israel: 'They are entangled in the land, and the wilderness hath shut them in'" (Exodus 14:3).

Moses/Akhenaten followed the instructions attributed to God and led the escapees on a route to the south into the Sinai, a place and route which would have been known to him from his many years in exile. We have already noted that Moses/Akhenaten would originally have been accompanied into exile, twenty-five years before the Exodus, by a coterie of persons that included military men. We know that the people leaving Egypt at the time of the Exodus constituted "a mixed multitude" (Exodus 12:38), which would have comprised Hebrews, Levites and other followers of Akhenaten/Moses. These followers would have likely included more military men and military engineers. Supporting this conclusion as to military capacity, the Torah, as already noted, states that the Hebrews were *armed*.

With respect to military strategy, the verses in Exodus 14:21-22 describe pillars of fire and smoke. The fire pots were normally placed at the front of the column, in the nature of a military guide-on, and the smoke was at the rear. However, as the Hebrews pretended to be boxed in against the waters (Exodus 14:3), the fire pots were moved for the night to the back of the column. From all appearances, the back became the front of the column. There were two reasons for doing this: First, the pursuing Egyptian force would then have believed that the Hebrews were facing them and preparing for a daylight confrontation and, second, the glare of the fire pots would have caused night blindness and permitted the Hebrews to leave at night from the far (or new back) side of the column without detection. Under the cover of darkness and with the aid of the fire-pot ruse, the Hebrews retreated across the water barrier. At this point, many of us are drawn to the image of the parting of the waters, as depicted in Cecil B. DeMille's film, "The Ten Commandments." I will submit another scenario.

In describing the ambush (and in rejecting DeMille's depiction of the parting waters), it is necessary to understand that the philosophy of Moses/Akhenaten rejects magic. Judaism parallels that approach. In Judaism, miracles reflect possibilities in and of laws of nature, not breaks in natural possibilities. So we must seek a scenario which must comply with physical possibilities. Second, we seek a predictable, not an unpredictable, physical possibility. This allows us to discount several competing explanations for the parting of the Yam Suph (also called the Sea of Reeds/Red Sea). For example, neither a shifting of waters resulting from an earthquake and a resulting tsunami-type wave nor, alternatively, a strong sustained wind would have been predictable in such a manner as to permit advance planning of military maneuvers.

The issue of the wind is particularly interesting because the text of the Torah refers in Exodus 15:8-10 to sustained winds. On this subject, C. Andrews published a study in 2010 entitled, "Dynamics of Wind Setdown at Suez and the Eastern Nile Delta." Summarizing his results, it would appear that a strong northeast wind, sustained for a period of twelve hours at 100 kilometers per hour (62 mph), would move the waters of a waterway enough to permit exposure of a walkway for a period of approximately four hours. Therefore, while the Torah makes references to the wind, it is unlikely that reality would have resembled a scene like that of Cecil B. DeMille because the dynamics would have required a sustained wind storm for an unrealistic period of time. When we factor in the suitability (and condition) of a newly exposed sea floor as a passable roadway and the ability to travel by foot in a wind of that strength, a near hurricane-force windstorm is an unrealistic scenario.

Before identifying the location of the Yam Suph, it is necessary to understand that, years before the life of Moses/Akhenaten, when the pyramids were built, stone blocks were transported from the quarries to the building sites through a series of canals built for that purpose.

Further evidence that the Egyptians were very knowledgeable regarding canals and irrigation is the fact that the patriarch Joseph had built a canal known as Joseph's Canal. This is a canal system in Egypt that parallels the Nile River and brings water to an oasis south of Cairo.[j] The Egyptians did not regard the parallel waterway as being ordinary; they reverently referred to it as the Bahr Youseff, which more accurately means "the Sea of Joseph." The canal system was possibly built as an irrigation system to mitigate the seven years of drought recited in the Torah and which was foretold by the patriarch Joseph to the pharaoh. Apropos the canals is a comment contained in the liner notes for the Philip Glass opera

---

[j] In the late nineteenth century, an American engineer named Francis Cope Whitehouse followed the traces of one canal. He found that the canal led to an artificial lake and discovered that the canal system also paralleled the Nile for several hundred kilometers.

"Akhnaten." The commentator, Shalom Goldman, writing of the historical background of the opera, discusses the Nile River and the use of man-made canals to allow continuous farming and agricultural activity in ancient Egypt: "The complex series of canals dug to facilitate irrigation had to be maintained and controlled by a strong central authority, personified by the king."[9]

Another example of waterway engineering is the large lake Amenhotep III (Akhenaten's father) created in Goshen for the enjoyment of his wife, Queen Tiye.

With respect to waterways, Brent MacDonald of Lion Tracks Ministries in Lutes Mountain, NB, Canada, provides a fascinating, plausible and, more importantly, predictable scenario for crossing the body of water referred to in the Torah as "Yam Suph." MacDonald convincingly identifies the Yam Suph as being an area with enough fresh water to permit growth of reeds. He identifies two former, but now dried up, canals which, at right angles, would have appeared to have to hemmed in the Hebrews. There was a north-south canal, which defined the eastern border of Egypt, called the Samana Canal. It was 10 feet deep, 200 feet wide and approximately 40 to 50 miles long. It extended from Lake Timsah on the south to the Pelusiac arm of the Nile River, effectively exiting into the Mediterranean on the north. This Samana Canal apparently served, in part, as a defensive wall against invaders. The Samana Canal also contained watchtowers to provide further defense. Interestingly, the Samana Canal not only prevented invaders from coming *into*, but also prevented dissidents from easily *exiting from* the land of Egypt. When the pharaoh relented and said in Exodus 12:31, "Go and be gone," he may very well have meant: "I give you permission to take your people through the established roads permitting exit from the country of Egypt." He would have meant the coastal road on the north.

There was also an east-west canal on the southern side of Goshen, extending from Lake Timsah on the east to the Nile River on the west. This canal existed in the depression called the Wadi (meaning valley) Tumilat. The Wadi Tumilat Canal was, apparently, a trench about 10 to 15 feet deep and about 150 feet wide. From east to west, it was approximately 100 miles in length. Also it is notable that, geographically and from the sense of the Torah text, the junction of the two canals was likely situated at or near Lake Timsah.

Time magazine, in an October 20, 1975, article, "Science: The First Suez Canal?" reported the discovery of such canals:

> While studying aerial photographs of the Nile Delta after their country's 1967 conquest of the Sinai, Israeli geologists noticed soil markings that were clearly vestiges of two dried-up waterways. One was quickly identified as a silted offshoot of the Nile River called the Pelusiac branch (after the ancient city of Pelusium at its mouth). The nature of the other waterway baffled the geologists until they visited the area and found man-made embankments. With that, they realized that these old mounds marked the route of a remarkable ancient canal that predated the Suez Canal by as many as 4,000

years. …

The old waterway probably ranged in depth from 7 ft. to 10 ft., adequate for ancient barges, but the embankments were 200 ft. apart, much wider than necessary for the water traffic of that day. The Israeli scientists think they know why. Writing in *American Scientist*, they point out that a wide channel would have made it an effective barrier against invaders from the east, a constant threat to ancient Egypt. In addition, it would have provided essential irrigation water. Could the ancient Egyptians have built such a great canal? Yes, say the geologists. After all, hundreds of year earlier the Egyptians had already tackled another project of comparable magnitude: the construction of their first pyramids.

Further, Morris Silver, of the Economics Department of the City of College of New York, speaks to the likelihood of locks existing in the canals:

That Egypt in the days of the Pharaohs was able to mass material and intellectual resources and make very significant technical achievements in the realm of water control cannot be doubted. … Cheryl Ward, Archaeological Director of the Institute of Nautical Archaeology in Egypt, informs me that

Using a cofferdam to close off an area from water either after hauling or floating a ship into it or building a ship in it (with or without stone foundations) and then cutting the dam is the simplest (and I believe most likely) way to maneuver immense weights (monoliths up to 740 tons and more) on and off watercraft. No representative, literary or archaeological evidence exists to support this practice from the pharaonic period, however. All we have is the Hatshepsut obelisk reliefs, where two 330-ton obelisks are loaded end to end on a ship that had to be 300 feet long and about 100 feet wide.

… The Wadi Tumilat and the eastern lakes area are natural depressions. The Wadi provided more than adequate water for navigation during the time of inundation. Locks placed appropriately at both ends of the Wadi Tumilat would have permitted the cargo vessels of the time to make a continuous journey by water to and from the Red Sea.[10]

The above reference to Queen Hatshepsut is significant. She ruled as pharaoh in the Eighteenth Dynasty, and *before* Amenhotep III and Akhenaten, his son. Therefore, any evidence that substantiates implied, or earlier express, construction and usage of dams and canals is relevant here.

Reference was earlier made to Lake Timsah. There is evidence that some of the commercial canal traffic used Lake Timsah as an area for transshipping (offloading and loading) commercial cargos. Lake Timsah was apparently shallow and, accordingly, dams would have been required to maintain the height of the lake, whether by draining the lake when it was flooded or to filling it when it had receded.

It should be remembered that Moses/Akhenaten had twenty-five years of exile within which to familiarize himself and his military engineers with the terrain of the area. Moses/Akhenaten and his military engineers could easily have planned to use, or build, a portage site across one of the two arms of the canals. It should also be remembered that usage of chariots as a separate arm of the Egyptian military had been developed by Yuya/Joseph, the grandfather of Moses/Akhenaten. While Moses/Akhenaten was not himself a military man, his military advisers and engineers, because of chariot tactics developed by Yuya/Joseph, would have had insight as to the strengths and weaknesses of the charioteers. Specifically, they would have known that a frontal assault on chariots would have led to devastating defeat. But there were weaknesses in the use of chariots. They had a relatively wide turn radius. The military advisers would have known that an attack on chariots would be required to come, effectively, from the sides, or flanks, of the charioteers.

Having set the stage for the confrontation with the pursuing forces of Ramses I, we must now further deal with engineering issues relating to the confrontation and planned ambush of the Egyptian forces.

With respect to maintenance of the canals, one would be required to assume that, where the terrain had areas of high ground and of low ground, a breach in any canal wall could have resulted in an uncontrolled emptying of all of the water of the waterway, unless there were periodic dams erected for water containment or flood relief. Further, the top of any such dam would have provided an ideal roadway from one side of the canal to the other. From a military point of view, these kinds of dams/roadways would have permitted a pharaonic defensive force to cross to the other side of the canal for purposes of attacking an invading force. It is likely that engineers would have built any dam/roadway structure somewhat below the surface to permit the passage of boat traffic and, further, to prevent an invading army from readily seeing the (subsurface) structure. If there were no suitable dam/roadway structure already located at the planned Exodus crossing location, Moses/Akhenaten and his military engineers could have easily built such a structure because, as noted above, the depth of the Samana Canal was only approximately 10 feet and the depth of the Wadi Tumilat Canal was no more than 15 feet. Constructing such a dam/roadway would not have been a problem, because the Hebrews had been the source of building the Egyptian storehouses in Goshen. They had the skill and numbers to complete such a construction project.

The series of diagrams/drawings in Appendix IV, depicts how and where Moses/Akhenaten and his military engineers could have used or erected a cofferdam or dams for military purposes and for providing a pathway for escape of the Hebrews.

The Hebrews would have crossed at night. Perhaps, as suggested by the Torah, the evening breezes would have exposed the surface of the dam/roadway. More likely, Moses and his military engineers would have bled the waters through sluices in a nearby area of depression to reduce the level of the waters on either side of the cofferdams. This would have allowed the Hebrews to walk on a dry surface and minimized the possibility that they inadvertently marched into the body of water on either side of the roadway. In any event, as the morning approached and the passage by the Hebrews had been completed, the Hebrews could have obstructed or walled off the east end of the roadway. The Hebrews would have established a reserve force on the near (western) side of the waters to act as tenders of the fire pots during the night and to act as a possible military line. Also, they would have established a military contingent to protect the people as they finished crossing to the far (eastern) side of the waters.

The pursuing Egyptian chariots would have been required to negotiate the exposed narrow roadway. That roadway would have permitted only a limited number of chariots and charioteers to cross at any one time; the balance of the charioteers would have been stuck in line on the far shore of the roadway itself. The chariots would have been effectively boxed in because the obstructions on the east side of the roadway would have prevented the chariots and charioteers from being able to regroup in any kind of formal military phalanx. By being stuck on the narrow roadway, the charioteers could not have reversed position because the turn radius of the chariots would have prevented that action.

The walls of the canal could then have been breached, at an area of depression, to empty the waters on both sides of the dam/roadway. If, as seems likely, Moses/Akhenaten arranged or built the roadway to face into the sun (being the Aten), the visual ability of the Egyptians to reconnoiter would have been limited by the blinding rays of the sun. As the waters subsided on both sides of the roadway because of the breached canal walls, a large-scale release of waters, from one of the cofferdams and, perhaps, from or into Lake Timsah as well, would have crashed into the roadway structure. That rush of water might have even begun to cover the roadway, as is suggested in the Torah. The military engineers of Moses/Akhenaten would have designed, or redesigned, the dam/roadway structure to react poorly to hydrostatic pressure against the structure resulting from waters rushing into the previously emptied canal. Such pressure upon the dam/roadway, unsupported by water pressure from the other side of the dam/roadway (now remaining emptied of water), would have impaired the integrity of the structure. At some point, hydrostatic pressure would have caused the impaired roadway to break. "Then the Lord *overthrew* the Egyptians in the *midst of the sea*" (Exodus 14:27). Further, "the horse and his rider [God] hath, *thrown* into the sea. … Pharaoh's chariots and his hosts hath he *cast* into the sea, and his chosen captains are *sunk* in the Yam Suph" (Exodus 15:1-4, emphasis added). The trapped Egyptians would have all drowned. The text and analysis of the Song of the Sea (Exodus 15:1-18) and the Song of Miriam (Exodus 15:19-21) are set forth in Appendix III. The text and song will be more fully reviewed and analyzed in Chapter Eight.

The Talmud supports the verse that suggests the death of Pharaoh Ramses I. It reports the Pharaoh as saying, "The law requires the soldier to advance in battle, even in the front of the conflict, but on this occasion I will lead and ye shall follow me. The law commands the king's servants to prepare his chariot, but see, this day I will prepare it myself."[11] Further, if for any reason some of the Egyptians had survived, the *armed* guard on either side of the canal would have been in a position to kill all or many of the stragglers. It is perhaps more than merely coincidental that Pharaoh Ramses I only reigned for approximately two years, a period of time sufficient to encompass the confrontations with the pharaoh, the ambush and the drowning.

It is also perhaps significant that, upon the death of Pharaoh Ramses I, his son and successor Pharaoh Seti I set out to attack the "Shasu" (who are commonly thought to be synonymous with the Hebrews) *before* the period of embalmment and mummification of his father and *before* he had been crowned as the successor pharaoh. Apparently, he was so enraged by the circumstance of his father's death that he immediately went into a battle mode to exact revenge for the death of his father.

The foregoing analysis corroborates the report of events in the Torah regarding the defeat of the pursuing Egyptian force and the drowning of Pharaoh Ramses I. Further, based upon the foregoing, it appears that we can specifically date the Exodus to the year 1333 BCE, being the year of death of Ramses I.

Naysayers might reject the foregoing description of an ambush because there are no apparent remains of chariots (such as wheels). However, this is readily explained. Seti I immediately followed to recover the body of his deceased father in order to prepare for the rites of mummification. In order to satisfy and quell the grief of the dead charioteers and to provide a degree of "closure" to affected families, the bodies of all of the dead charioteers would have similarly been recovered. The chariots, shields and spears would have been recovered for further use and to prevent the Hebrews (or other potential adversaries) from collecting them for future attacks against the regime(s) of the Nineteenth Dynasty.

There is more proof of the deluge. But before dealing with that additional proof, we should examine the size of the Exodus population. The Torah indicates that 600,000 men left Egypt. Multiplying that group by a figure that would include women and children results in approximately 1.5 million to 2 million people. These numbers are logically unsupportable and present yet another instance in the Torah where numbers are distorted.

There are multiple texts which indicate that the word "eleph," which is commonly translated as "one thousand" and which is used in the Torah (in the aforesaid computation of 600,000), can also be translated as "group" or "clan." In that regard, there are several references in Deuteronomy (7:1, 9:1, 11:23 and 20:1) that indicate that the Hebrews were not as large a nation as the non-Hebrew tribes around them. Recomputation and recalculation, using the word eleph as group or clan (rather than as one thousand) results in a total population of the "mixed multitude" of the Exodus as comprising a much smaller number of people. It is more likely that the escaping force consisted of 20,000 men at the most.

Similarly, Exodus 14:7 states that the pharaoh assembled a group of more than 600 chariots. If a chariot and horse amounted to a length of approximately 15 feet, a line or grouping of 600 chariots would have been, effectively, a logistic impossibility. Therefore, it is more likely that the pharaoh would have assembled a smaller, more maneuverable force of about 60 to 100 chariots.

Returning to the issue of a deluge, proof of same is, perhaps, further corroborated by Simcha Jacobovici (The Naked Archeologist), who photographed tombstone markings in the form of water waves at Mycenae on mainland Greece for his television production concerning the Exodus. The tombstones seem to reflect that a group of Hebrews left Egypt at the time of the Exodus and that, rather than proceeding east into the Sinai Peninsula with the largest group of escaping Hebrews, they sailed to Mycenae for refuge. Such a splitting of the Hebrew camp is not without apparent precedent. (In this regard, please refer to the text regarding the journey of ancestors of the Irish and Scotch peoples being apparent followers of Pharaoh Aye.)

An article by Steven M. Collins relates to both the number of Hebrews and the possible movement by some of the peoples of the Exodus to Greece. He analyzes the census numbers and notes that the numbers of Hebrews in the tribes of Simeon, Ephraim and Naphtali were substantially decreased in census totals between the first and second census countings:

> The most evident change is that over half the tribe of Simeon inexplicably "disappeared" from the census totals. What happened? Simeon, the third largest tribe in Israel in the first census, had plummeted to be the smallest tribe of all in the second census! …
>
> I believe the key to what happened in Numbers 26 is found in the previous chapter. In Numbers 25 … a Levite executed 'a prince of a chief house among the Simeonites' (verses 7-14). …
>
> It is my belief that after the execution of a Simeonite prince by a Levitical priest, there was a great dissension in the camp of Israel. We know from the accounts in the Torah … that the Israelites were very prone to revolting against Moses over various provocations … and a civil war among the tribes was not improbable. …
>
> I believe…that most of the tribe of Simeon and varying contingents of the other tribes literally 'walked out' of the camp and left the main body of Israelites to strike out on their own. …
>
> Would God or Moses have allowed so large a mass of Israelites to leave the camp? I think the answer is yes. Indeed they may have encouraged this as a way to end the dissension in the camp. …
>
> There is a group … famous in the ancient world, which exhibited the traits of Simeon and which acknowledged a tribal tie to the Israelites. That group

was the Spartans of ancient Greece. The Spartans were known to be descended from a people non-native to Greece who arrived there in ancient times. … They had a rigorous, martial community which was very different from the rest of the Greek city-states. The tribe of Simeon would be expected to be a martial community where they settled. …

The book 'Sparta,' by A.H.M. Jones, a Professor of Ancient History at Cambridge University, noted several things about Sparta. He states the Spartans worshipped a 'great law-giver' who had given them their laws in the 'dim past.' This law-giver may have been Moses. …

Interestingly … the Spartans were themselves divided into several 'tribes' which constituted distinct military formations within the Spartan army. If the Spartans were descended from Simeonites and several other Israelite tribes who left the rest of their tribesmen just prior to the census of Numbers 26, it would make sense that they would be allied together as distinct tribes even in a new homeland like Sparta.

I have saved the greatest proof to the last, however. The Spartans themselves declared that they were a fellow tribe of the Jews and corresponded with an ancient Jewish High Priest about their relationship. The book of I Maccabees 14:16-23 records this correspondence which includes this statement:

> And this is the copy of the letter which the Spartans sent: The Chief magistrates and the city of the Spartans send greeting to Simon, the chief priest, and to the elders and the priests and the rest of the Jewish people, our kinsmen.

Notice the Spartans called the Jews 'our Kinsmen.' The Spartans did not proclaim themselves to be Jews, but rather that they were 'kinsmen' to the Jews (i.e. members of one of the other tribes of Israel). That the Spartans acknowledged a common ancestry with the Jews of the tribe of Judah gives powerful weight to the assertion that they were Israelites who migrated to Greece instead of the Promised Land. The Spartan culture is most like that of the tribe of Simeon, most of which apparently left the Israelite encampment in the Wilderness after a Simeon prince was executed by a Levite.[12]

The analysis by Collins is supported by the Torah story of the rape of Dinah and the vengeful killing of Hivites from Genesis 34. This Torah story sets forth retribution, by Simeon and Levi, for the rape of their sister. Collins' position is further supported by the deathbed blessings of Jacob in Genesis 49:5, where Jacob again castigates Simeon and Levi because of their violence. He states that the descendants of Simeon will be dispersed, perhaps in the manner suggested by Collins, and that the descendants of Levi will be dispersed among the other tribes. The Levites would not have lands of their own.

Using the recalculation method suggested above, the numbers of Hebrews in the tribes of Simeon, Ephraim and Naphtali would be reduced from 53,000 to approximately 1,000. If we multiply the 1,000 men by wives and children, there would be approximately 2,000 to 2,500 people, being approximately 6.5 percent of the total camp. This is still a substantial exodus from the camp, but would more rationally track the movements of the peoples who were involved in such apparent exodus to the Greek mainland.

Collins' analysis is interesting for another reason. It may relate the possibility of an earlier transfer of Hebrews of the Exodus to Mycenae to suggested relocation by Collins of part of the tribes of Simeon, Ephraim and Napthali to Sparta. Both groups would have shared a common heritage, which might have caused them to pick sites for relocation that were close to each other. These two locations are, in fact, geographically close; that proximity may lend a further degree of credence to the stories of both relocations.

Conversely, the fact that two groups of Hebrews had left the body of the main group may have resulted in a competitive, and semi-hostile, relationship between the Hebrews and the ancient Greeks. We will further discuss this matter in Chapter Seven, and also in a discussion of prohibited sexual relations at the end of Appendix VII.

Whatever the case, the main body of Hebrews had successfully left Egypt, the land of oppression. It is time to discuss the results of that Exodus.

7

SUBSTANCE OF
A NEW RELIGION

Records of the respective early histories of Akhenaten and Moses are weighted heavily in favor of those of Akhenaten. It would appear that this is true for two reasons. First, despite the efforts of the Pharaoh of Oppression, Horemheb, to eradicate all traces of Akhenaten and prohibit the verbal or written expression of his full proper name, much archaeological record of Akhenaten remains. In fact, Horemheb unwittingly helped to preserve these records. When Horemheb became pharaoh, he caused much of the remaining buildings and monuments erected by Akhenaten/Moses to be destroyed. In city of Akhetaten, Horemheb caused much of the debris to be buried on site so that little physical evidence of the city was apparent to the naked eye; however, burying of the building materials in the dry climate of Egypt actually preserved relevant inscriptions and murals. Second, when the Torah was later reduced to writing, relationships between Akhenaten and Moses were fudged. For example, we should consider the intense rivalries within the Hebrew encampment. Frictions existed between Moses and Aaron. Frictions existed between Moses (and Aaron) and Pinchas (Phineas). Finally, frictions existed between Moses and Aaron, on the one hand, and the rest of the Hebrews, on the other hand. All of these historical matters of conflict were blurred in writing the Torah. To the contrary, in the Torah, explanation of the enterprise of creating a new religion was attributed to the actions of God.

As earlier stated, I do not denigrate the existence of a supreme being. However, in order to understand the shear magnitude and grandeur of the religious innovations and creations of Moses/Akhenaten, as well as the civil and social unrest caused thereby, it is necessary to review these innovations and creations in a historical setting. In order to better highlight these subjects, for the balance of this chapter, I will insert topic headings in an outline form.

Before further proceeding, the reader should recognize that I am not saying that Moses/Akhenaten accomplished all of these innovations and creations by himself or at one time. He and his Levite companions did accomplish certain things immediately. But, perhaps more importantly, they also set a stage that permitted and engendered a further evolution of the matters set forth below. Some of these matters resulted from conflicts between the Levites and Moses/Akhenaten; in some circumstances, Moses prevailed, in others, the Levites were the prevailing party.

I. The Historical Beginnings of Mosaic Judaism

As has already been noted, there was a strong symbiotic relationship between the Hebrews and the ancient Egyptians. This may have begun with the relationship between Abraham, Sarah and a pharaoh and continued with relationships behind the biblical story of the "Binding of Isaac." We will address these issues and relationships later.

More directly, as noted in Chapter Three, Pharaoh Tuthmosis IV appointed Yuya/Joseph as his vizier (prime minister); Yuya/Joseph retained that title and capacity with the next pharaoh, Amenhotep III. When Yuya/Joseph became vizier, he married an Egyptian wife, Tuya. Tuya was not a Hebrew. Their daughter, Tiye, and their sons were not Hebrews. That is because Judaism was not, at that time, an organized or institutionalized religion and because the religious affiliation of a child was determined by matriarchal descent (i.e. by the religion of the mother). If the brothers of Yuya/Joseph had not come to Egypt to obtain relief from severe famine, Yuya/Joseph would likely have lived his life without any further Hebrew identification. It was only when his brothers appeared in Egypt that the ties between Yuya/Joseph and his family were restored. As a result, he caused his father, Jacob, to be brought to Egypt. By the time his father died, Yuya/Joseph had regained enough Hebrew identification to have the remains of his father returned to Canaan for burial. This action indicated two things: 1) there was, even then, a historical relationship between the Hebrews and the land of Canaan; and 2) there appear to have been Hebrews still living in Canaan who had not descended into Egypt. However, the religion could have easily died with Yuya/Joseph and his brothers, except for one thing. Yuya/Joseph had a grandson, Moses/Akhenaten.

As we have noted, when Moses/Akhenaten was born, there was an effort, largely promoted by the priests of Amun, to have him killed. He was protected and raised by (or through the efforts of) his mother, Queen Tiye, who was herself of Hebrew descent. (Again, Queen Tiye was technically not a member of the Hebrew religion because, as noted, her mother, Tuya, was not a Hebrew.) In fact, an examination of the actions of Queen Tiye shows that her actions were apparently not motivated by religion. She merely wanted to ensure that her progeny would reign as pharaohs and that they would continue to bear the Egyptian crown. Therefore, Queen Tiye sent Moses/Akhenaten to live with her relatives in Goshen to protect the dynasty and her position in it. However, in Goshen, Moses/Akhenaten would have absorbed at least a rudimentary knowledge of a monotheistic outlook of the Hebrews of Goshen, as well as their customs and language. After his older brother Tuthmosis died (or was assassinated), his father, Amenhotep III, turned to him as his only apparent male heir through his Great Royal Wife, Queen Tiye, to perpetuate the dynasty. Again, while religion and kingship were normally determined by *matriarchal* descent, kingship generally passed to a *male* heir. To promote his ascension to the throne, Akhenaten/Moses was brought from Goshen to Thebes where he was exposed to the theology of the Amunite priesthood.

Despite the hostility of the Amunite priests to Akhenaten/Moses at his birth, Akhenaten/Moses sought their acceptance and approval. When they continued to reject him, he reverted to his Hebrew memories and beliefs of and in a single God, and, in a reversal of roles, *he rejected the Amunite priesthood and its theology.* He began to expand his emotional and intellectual acceptance of a monotheistic religious outlook. He identified his concept of a single god with worship of Aten, the sun god. This was an easy step for him because his father, Amenhotep III, had interwoven an Atenistic theology with the more common theological beliefs in Amun. In fact, the name of the royal barge, which was built by Amenhotep III for the pleasure of Queen Tiye, could be translated as "Aten Gleams" or "God is Radiant."

Moses/Akhenaten portrayed his god pictorially as a falcon-man. His belief that the sun god was the provider of all life was, in fact, reflective of the modern science of biology. We now know that the sun allows plants to create chlorophyll through photosynthesis; without this biological process, there would be no life as we know it. Moses/Akhenaten, in his theological reliance on the sun as the source of life, proceeded to a complete rejection of the cult of Osiris. Osiris was the god of the afterlife and the judge of the dead; effectively, Osiris ruled in, and at, darkness. Darkness, obviously, is the antithesis of light. Previous pharaohs were associated with Osiris in the pharaonic quest for an afterlife. When Osiris arose from death, the dead pharaohs would arise in unison from death for perpetual life, thus effecting their resurrection.

The Amunite theology related, in effect, to gods of daytime and daylight and Osiris as the god of night. Akhenaten/Moses rejected this theology and substituted the concept of a single God as to which he (and later each of his followers) would interrelate on all aspects of living.

II. Worldly Theology

The rejection of the cult of Osiris resulted in a worldly, as opposed to an oth-er-worldly, view of theology. This quantum leap in the religious belief of Moses/Akhenaten was carried into Judaism and is reflected in institutionalized Judaism by the lack of a definitive view of heaven or hell. In Judaism, a person is required to act properly because it is the right thing to do, rather than acting properly because of a promise of heaven or a threat of eternal hell or damnation. Moses/Akhenaten showed this religious development pictorially by eliminating the falcon-man as the representation of Aten and substituting a representation of godhead with a non-animal, non-human portrayal of Aten as a sun disc only. It is perhaps signifi-cant that the circular figure similar to a sun disc was maintained as a sign of royalty by subsequent Hebrew kings. It was called a "Lamelech" sign, the word Lamelech meaning "to the King."

The further development of Jewish theological conceptions of heaven and hell and an afterlife is considered by Alfred J. Kolatch. He notes that:

> The Bible makes no direct reference to a heaven or hell as a place to which people go after death. Chapters 2 and 3 of Genesis as well as Chapter 28 of Ezekiel refer to an earthly Garden of Eden (Gan Ayden in Hebrew), but this is not the celestial paradise referred to in later Jewish literature. Only after the destruction of the First Temple in 586 B.C.E. and the subsequent exile of Jews to Babylonia (later conquered by Persia), at which time Jews came under the strong influence of Persian Zoroastrian teachings, did the concept of heaven and hell become the subject of serious discussion among Jews. ...
>
> Scholars of post-Talmudic centuries were less and less inclined to view the hereafter as a physical place. Gan Ayden to Rabbi Moses ben Nachman (Nachmanides) of the thirteenth century was a 'world of souls' (olam hane-shamot in Hebrew). It was a place where only the souls, not the bodies, of the departed would enter immediately after death. Maimonides, a century earlier, wrote: 'There are neither bodies nor bodily forms in the world-to-come, only the souls of the righteous.' ...
>
> Most Jews today, Orthodox and non-Orthodox, believe in the immortality of the soul, but not all believe in paradise and hell and the physical resurrec-tion of the dead. Reform Judaism and Reconstructionism accept only the idea of immortality of the soul, and their prayer books reflect this attitude.[1]

In considering the comments of Kolatch, one should note that Moses/Akhenaten would have been highly critical of any belief in paradise, hell and the physical resurrection of the dead.

III. Miracles as Part of Natural Order

Akhenaten/Moses also rejected acceptance of, and religious reliance on, imitative priestly magic. This is again carried into Judaism by the rejection in Judaism of miracles as an extra-physical force. In Judaism, miracles may be extra-ordinary happenstances, but they are never adduced in support of the faith. This view is further set forth by Kolatch. He notes that miracles:

> …were not miracles in the sense that we understand the word. The biblical happenings that we call miracles were actually preordained events that were programmed into nature and were thus part of the natural order. Accordingly, the miracles of the Bible were no longer to be considered a break with the natural order, but a fulfillment of a plan that was set in motion at the very beginning.[2]

In this regard, the stories in the Torah, such as in Exodus 4:2-9 relating the conversion of Moses' staff into a serpent, telling the story of the white or leprous hand, describing the conversion of the waters of the Nile to blood and, later, in Exodus 7:8-12, relating the magical swallowing of the pharaonic staffs by the rod or staff of Aaron, must be considered in a non-magical setting. As Osman says:

> We know also that Akhenaten rejected all kinds of magic. …

> When we examine the acts said to have been performed by Moses to establish his identity, we find that they are largely related to some old Egyptian rituals that kings used to perform at their *sed* festivals for the purpose of rejuvenating their power.

> The Koran gives a slightly different account of this confrontation, an account which contains more significant details that are to be found in the [Torah] and is in closer agreement with the earlier details in the Book of Exodus. …

> This section of the Koran presents the confrontation in such a precise way that one wonders if some of the details were left out of the biblical account deliberately. Here Moses sounds less like a magician, more like someone who presents evidence of his authority that convinces the wise men of Egypt, who throw themselves at his feet and thus earn the punishment of the Pharaoh. One can only suspect that the biblical editor exercised care to avoid any Egyptian involvement with the Israelite Exodus, even to the extent of replacing Moses by Aaron in the performance of the rituals. …

> No magic was performed, or intended, by Moses. The true explanation of the biblical story could only be that it was relating the political challenge for power in a mythological way — and all the plagues of which we read were natural, seasonal events in Egypt in the course of every year.[3]

The rejection of priestly magic and miracles as an extra-physical force is relevant to the earlier analysis of the story of the drowning of Pharaoh Ramses I. In this context, the real miracles of that story were, first, that the Exodus from Egypt was successful and, second, that the religion of Moses/Akhenaten and of the Levites survived and evolved to the forms of Judaism that exist today.

IV. Ethical Monotheism

Akhenaten proceeded from polytheism to monotheism. But, of greater significance, his monotheism developed into *ethical* monotheism. This is the very crux and heart of the theology of Moses/Akhenaten. It is perceived in several manners.

A. Ten Commandments

A form of ethical theology is displayed in Spell 125 of the Egyptian "Book of the Dead." This spell contains Negative Confessions containing, as related by Osman,[4] assurances among other such declarations of a deceased person that:

I have done no falsehood,

I have not robbed,

I have not stolen,

I have not killed men,

I have not told lies.

Moses/Akhenaten converts the passive Negative Confessions to mandatory requirements, as set forth in the Ten Commandments:

I am the Lord thy God.

Thou shalt have no other Gods before me; Thou shalt not make for thyself an idol.

Thou shalt not take the name of the Lord thy god in vain.

Remember the Sabbath day and keep it holy.

Honor thy father and mother.

Thou shalt not murder.

Thou shalt not commit adultery.

Thou shalt not steal.

Thou shalt not bear false witness against thy neighbor.

Thou shalt not covet the house or wife of thy neighbor.

An examination of the Ten Commandments indicates several interesting matters. First, Moses/Akhenaten ratifies the action of Abraham in rejecting the idols of Abraham's father. This is demonstrated by Moses/Akhenaten's action of changing the representation of God from a falcon-man to that of a non-animal, non-human and non-corporeal God.

When I was in grammar school, my recollection is that our history book, in connection with the history of Western Civilization, had a single comment about Judaism. The book stated that Judaism gave to the world, solely, the belief in a single God. That approach was incorrect. One of the glaring proofs that this was not the sole contribution of Judaism is the mandate and commandment that all humankind is to have a weekly day set aside for rest and study, but not for the performance of work. We will consider other contributions of Judaism later in this chapter.

The requirement that "one shall honor" thy father and mother is fascinating. This mandate is psychologically very insightful; it leaps into modern psychoanalytical concepts and practice. The requirement is not that one must love, like, obey, support, or respect one's parents. It merely requires that one is to give *deference* to his or her parents; this permits each person (as a child or descendant) to "honor" his or her parents, while permitting a separate accommodation or flexibility as to the degree of positive or negative emotional interaction between a child and his or her parent(s).

The entire issue of converting the passive Negative Confessions of the Egyptian "Book of the Dead," which may merely reflect the lack of a challenge during the life of a person (to avoid acting in a negative manner), to a mandatory requirement of action is central to Judaism. In Judaism, the motivation of the action is not critical, but the action itself is critical. For example, a person might have no personal relationship to a disabled person and, therefore, no reason to act charitably toward him or her. Resentment may even arise in the act of helping the disabled person. However, the *action* of giving aid, whether it is easily forthcoming or given with great reluctance and resentment, is the requirement. Regardless of the motivation, a keystone of Judaism is that people are responsible for taking positive actions; that is *ethical* monotheism.

B. Freedom

In leaving Egypt, the Hebrews effected their freedom from the evil, forced labor and mental enslavement of the Pharaoh of Oppression, Horemheb. But, as Louis Finkelstein points out, the Exodus generated a unique kind of freedom. It:

> commemorates an event which will probably symbolize for all time the essential meaning of freedom — namely, freedom directed to a purpose. When Israel came forth from bondage, it was not simply to enjoy liberty, but to make of liberty an instrument of service. There have been countless other emancipations of subject peoples. … But none of these other emancipations acquired any ethical significance. None of these peoples have left records interpreting their liberation as a means to a higher end, and therefore none of them helped develop any spiritual ideals as a result of their early experience. The Israelites alone made the moment of their origin as a people one of permanent self-dedication to the principle of universal freedom as the essential prerequisite for spiritual growth. Hence the event has meaning for all living peoples.[5]

C. Offshoots of Ethical Monotheism

While the concept of Tzedakah, or charity, evolved at a later time in the Torah and Talmud texts, the giving of aid to people in need is a natural evolution of ethical monotheism and the commandments that one shall not steal nor covet the possessions of one's neighbors. In fact, those two commandments are themselves an evolution from the story of Cain killing Abel, when Cain questions God, "Am I my brother's keeper?" While that question is never directly answered, the subtext is that, yes, we are all our brothers' keepers. We have an earthly responsibility to maintain the common good. The concept of charity is a natural extension of these principles. This is so important to the Jewish religion, whether in ancient or in modern times, that it is almost commonplace or axiomatic. For example, after the 2004 Indonesian earthquake and tsunami, one of the first responders, in terms of various forms of aid and assistance, was the State of Israel, which immediately sent water, provisions and medical supplies to Sri Lanka and Indonesia. Later, after the 2010 Haitian earthquake, the Israel Defense Force or its affiliates (such as Magen David Adom, being the Jewish "Red Cross,") sent medical teams which immediately began medical treatment and assistance even though it was Friday evening, the beginning of the Sabbath, when work is normally prohibited. After the 2012 Turkey earthquake, the Israeli government offered, in spite of strained relationships between the governments of Turkey and Israel, to send support teams to Turkey.

D. Misogyny and the Treatment of Others

Misogyny, the hatred of women, has been characterized as a prominent feature of various religions. However, it is not a substantive part of Judaism. This probably results from the relationship between Akhenaten/Moses and Nefertiti/Miriam, who were betrothed when he was a young boy. Nefertiti/Miriam was of royal blood. As Osman points out, in quoting another writer, Winfield Smith:

> An astonishing emphasis on Nefertiti is demonstrated by the frequency of her name in the cartouches on offering tables, as contrasted with the relatively few cartouches of Amenhotep IV. The queen's name alone occurs sixty-seven times, whereas only thirteen tables carry both names, and a mere three show only the king's name. He goes on to discuss the appearance of statues of the king and queen on offering tables that appear on the *talalat*, the small stones used in building Akhenaten's Karnak temple and later re-used by Horemheb after the temple's destruction: "There are sixty-three Nefertiti statues and thirty-eight Amenhotep IV statues, with eleven unidentified. Significant is not only the preponderance of Nefertiti, but even more important the extraordinary domination of the larger offering tables by Nefertiti statues. It will be noticed that all of the five identified statues of the large size … are of Nefertiti." [6]

More importantly, Nefertiti/Miriam was the love of Akhenaten/Moses' life. The feeling was reciprocal; the strength of their relationship is treated in Chapter Eight. Suffice it to say, Nefertiti/Miriam was apparently a moderating force with respect to the emotions and actions of Akhenaten/Moses. The archaeological records seem to indicate that Akhenaten/Moses was the writer of the Hymn to Aten, described in greater detail below. Nefertiti/Miriam may have helped write this hymn. That form of assistance or cooperative effort is suggested by an analysis of the "Song of the Sea" as set forth in Exodus (Chapter 15:1-21) and in Chapter Eight. This song is attributed to Moses at the time of destruction of the Egyptian host in pursuit of the people of the Exodus at the Yam Suph. The Torah also attributes a second element of that song to Miriam/Nefertiti and many analysts contend that Miriam/Nefertiti wrote the text of *both* parts of that song.

Aside from Egyptian sources, the Torah establishes the strong historical relationship and support structure given by Miriam/Nefertiti to Moses/Akhenaten. First, Miriam/Nefertiti was present at the childhood (birth) of Moses. Second, she was present at the site of the Yam Suph at the time of destruction of the pursuing Egyptian host. Third, Miriam/Nefertiti was described as providing drinking water for the Hebrews in the desert. The relationship between Moses/Akhenaten and Miriam/Nefertiti displays nothing of hatred, degradation, or demonization of women.

In current times, it has become customary on the eve of the Sabbath for an observant husband to recite the "Eishet Chayil" to his wife. This is done before the Kiddush (being the blessing over the Sabbath cup of wine). It is an acknowledgment of the wife's important position as a mainstay of the household. It consists of the last twenty-two verses of the Book of Proverbs in alphabetical sequence. The words of the "Eishet Chayil" are:

> A good wife, who can find? Her worth is far above rubies. The heart of her husband trusts in her and nothing shall he lack. She renders him good and not evil all the days of her life. She opens her hand to the needy and she extends her hand to the poor. She is robed in strength and dignity and cheerfully faces whatever may come. She opens her mouth with wisdom, her tongue is guided by kindness. She tends to the affairs of her household and eats not the bread of idleness. Her children come forward and bless her, her husband, too, and he praises her: "Many women have done superbly, but you surpass them all."
>
> Charm is deceitful and beauty is vain, but a God-revering woman is much to be praised. Place before her the fruit of her hands; wherever people gather, her deeds speak her praise.[7]

While we can acknowledge that not every female is a person of goodness and equanimity, it is the general tone of the words that is so significant. The tone is one of great approval.

This section dealing with the subject of misogyny should not be taken as a denial of the fact that Hebrew women were faced with issues of subservience to men. It is not true to say that women were always treated on a par with men in Jewish history. In fact, one is required to acknowledge that women are not given primary positions in the Measharim area of Jerusalem or in certain other ultraorthodox areas of the current world. However, the accounts of the actions of Sarah (vis-a-vis Abraham), Rebecca, Rachel (vis-a-vis her father), Miriam/Nefertiti, Ruth, Naomi, the prophetess Deborah, Queen Esther and Judith of the Apocrypha show an elevated acceptance and appreciation of the position and contribution of women in Hebrew society. The election of Golda Meir as Prime Minister of the State of Israel is another example of the position of women in Jewish society. Again, the point of this section is that misogyny was not institutionalized as a religious principle of Judaism.

On a related note, not only were women treated in a positive and elevated manner, but also non-Hebrews. In repeated references in the Torah, the terms ger (singular) and gerim (plural) are used to indicate that strangers were to be treated with fairness and kindness. One example is set forth in Leviticus 19:33-34. "And if a stranger [ger] sojourned with thee in your land, ye shall not do him wrong. The stranger [ger] that sojourneth with you shall be unto you as the home born among you, and thou shalt love him as yourself, for ye were strangers [gerim] in the land of Egypt." Strangers were not to be humiliated, mistreated, or brutalized.

V. Molding of an Ethnic Group

Moses/Akhenaten understood that the survival of his religion depended upon his ability to mold a disparate group of people into a cohesive ethnic entity. This was not easy; sometimes it was met by harsh resistance. We see this in the many reported instances in the Torah of complaining by the Hebrews about their participation in the Exodus. Perhaps the most striking instance of conflict is the story of the rebellion of Korah (Numbers 16:1-35). Freidman not only reports the text of the story, but also dissects the story into the "JE" text and also the "P" text. He points out that the text really is about *two* challenges. First is the rebellion of Dathon and Abiram. This is a challenge to Moses' leadership. The second is from a group of Levites, led by Korah, who challenge Aaron's exclusive hold on the priesthood. Friedman concludes that: "The 'JE' story of the rebellion was a justification of Moses. But the Priestly version is a justification of Aaron."[8] In any event, the text is one of many instances in the Torah of complaining by, and of insubordination of, the Hebrews of the Exodus. Again, creating a cohesive ethnic entity was not easy.

A. Circumcision

Circumcision was an innovation of the Egyptian people. Moses/Akhenaten was apparently reluctant to accept circumcision as a rite of the Hebrews. In this regard, Moses/Akhenaten did not initially insist upon the circumcision of one of his sons, Tutankhamun. This is illustrated by a strange story in Exodus 4:23-26. God sought to *kill* Moses and, further, Zipporah (Queen Tiye) criticized Moses by saying: "Surely a bridegroom of blood art thou to me," followed by, "A bridegroom of blood in regard of the circumcision." There is no apparent further historical explanation of these verses. However, an examination of the two phrases, placed in close proximity to each other, discloses a distinction. In the first usage, there is no reference to circumcision. In the second usage, the reference is apparently restricted to circumcision. Certainly, there is an implication in the text of greater bloodshed than pertains to, or results from, the procedure of a circumcision. It may be that Queen Tiye (Zipporah) was repulsed by Akhenaten/Moses' use of military force against the Egyptian people in maintaining his kingship and reign. The repression of the people and attacks against the citizens of Egypt could have escalated into bloodshed. But the second expression of Queen Tiye was a direct reference to circumcision.

In any event, since that time and incident, circumcision is and remains an almost universal rite of Judaism.

B. Prohibited Sexual Relationships

In the middle of the Book of Leviticus (18:6), there is a list of prohibited sexual relationships. Hertz notes that: "There was dire need for legislation [as contained] in this chapter. Many of the incestuous marriages herein mentioned were common among contemporary peoples. ... In Egypt, marriage with a sister was quite usual, especially in royal families."[9] While Hertz does not make a connection between his comments and the brother-sister relationship between Moses/Akhenaten and Miriam/Nefertiti, the positioning of the text in the middle book of the Torah (Leviticus) and in the middle of that book, seems to set forth an implied strong criticism by the Torah writers to the incestuous sexual relationships maintained by Moses/Akhenaten with Miriam/Nefertiti and with Queen Tiye.

Earlier in this book, we noted that Charles Pope references the deliberate intermarriage between close members of the royal family for purposes of "genetic engineering." As will later appear, Aaron/Meryare II rejects the concept of genetic engineering through incest for apparently no less than three reasons. First, it is emotionally repugnant. Second, inbreeding results in a closed social system. The royalty is deliberately cut off from connection with the mass of its subjects; the gene pool is circumscribed and limited. Third, and most importantly, inbreeding results, rather than in genetically engineered perfection, in genetic defects and physical and medical disabilities. Again, the critical rejection of incestuous marriages and incestuous relationships were a direct indictment by the Levites of the incestuous sexual activities of Moses/Akhenaten.

C. Matriarchal Descent

We have noted that royalty passed in the Egyptian monarchy by descent to the son through the mother. This rule of matriarchal descent was carried over into Judaism. Generally (except in Reform Judaism), the religion of the mother determines the religion of the child. This rule is, perhaps, evidence of the elevated status of women in the religious fabric of Moses/Akhenaten.

D. Mikvah; Pools for Religious Purification

Immersion in water was and remains critical to monotheistic religions, including Judaism, Christianity and Islam. Significantly, Osman, in referring to the Temple area of Mount Sarabit (referred to in Chapter Six of this book) states that:

"At Sarabit there were three rectangular tanks and a circular basin, placed to be used at four different stages of entering the temple. This makes it clear that ablutions played a great role in the form of worship at Sarabit."[10]

The Mikvah was used to grant ritual purity to both male and female Hebrews. It was significant to the priesthood as well as the common Hebrews. The Mikvah has retained its significance in the modern world for Orthodox and (some) Conservative Jews.

E. Kashruth

Another identification of ethnicity relates to the distinctive diet of Jewish tradition. The term for religiously proper food preparation in the Jewish tradition is "kashruth" or keeping kosher. For several years at the end of the reign of Amenhotep III and continuing into the reign of Akhenaten, there had been a severe plague in Egypt. In Exodus 15:26, God says that: "If thou wilt diligently hearken to the voice of the Lord … I will put none of the diseases upon thee, which I have put upon the Egyptians." This verse would appear to presage institution of the laws of kashruth. Whether or not kashruth is fully related to keeping members of the Hebrew assemblage healthy and alive, the institution of kashruth (keeping kosher) defined Jewish ethnicity thereafter.

F. Personal Responsibility

There is never a clear distinction, whether given by God or whether determined by mankind, as to whether self-help is appropriate in a given situation. However, a passage in Exodus 14:11-15 indicates a requirement that mankind, in considered circumstances, should act affirmatively and in a positive manner, rather than in a passive manner:

v 11 And they said unto Moses: "Because there were no graves in Egypt, hast thou taken us away to die in the wilderness? Wherefore hast thou dealt thus with us, to bring us forth out of Egypt?"

v 12 Is not this the word that we spoke unto thee in Egypt, saying: "Let us alone, that we may serve the Egyptians? For it were better for us to serve the Egyptians, than that we should die in the wilderness."

v 13 And Moses said unto the people: "Fear ye not, stand still, and see the salvation of the Lord, which He will work for you to-day; for whereas ye have seen the Egyptians to-day, ye shall see them again no more for ever.

v 14 "The Lord will fight for you, and ye shall hold your peace."

v 15 And the Lord said unto Moses: "Wherefore criest thou unto Me? Speak unto the children of Israel, that they go forward."

Moses states that "the Lord will fight for you." However, God's response is striking: "Don't ask me; help yourselves and *move out!*" Again, while historically there are many, many times when it is better to "live for another day," rather than to die as a hero, this text presages the current posture of the people of the State of Israel. In the continuing spirit of the above Torah text, they *will* defend themselves.

G. Self Defense

The history of the Hebrews in Exodus is replete with instances of armed conflict. It is significant, for our purposes, to identify only a few of such reports. First, we have already noted that Exodus 13:18 states that: "The children of Israel went up *armed* out of the land of Egypt" (emphasis added). That circumstance relates to the later defeat at Yam Suph of the host of Egyptians pursuing the Israelites as they left the land of Egypt. Further, the census, reported in Numbers 1:1-46, sets forth a *military count*. The purpose of the census was to establish and encourage preparation for battle. Related to this census is a report in Numbers 10:1-2 about the creation of two trumpets made of silver. Verse 9 specifically states that "when ye go to war ... ye shall sound an alarm with the trumpets."

At the unearthing of artifacts from the tomb of Pharaoh Tutankhamun, there were two trumpets found, one made of silver and the other of copper. The silver trumpet is fully consistent with the above description in the biblical text about trumpets. What is perhaps more fascinating is that, if the reader searches the internet for "Tutankhamun" and "silver trumpet", the reader can *hear* a recording made of the actual sounding of the silver and copper trumpets found within Tutankhamun's tomb. Listening to that recording will give the reader a direct connection with the biblical text and bring to life the biblical sounds of 3,000 years ago.

Further, Deuteronomy 25:17-19 states: "Remember what Amalek did unto thee ... as ye came forth out of Egypt. ... Therefore ... thou shalt blot out the remembrance of Amalek from under the heaven; thou shalt not forget." Later, in Jewish history, the Hasmonean family of Judah Maccabee defeated the Seleucid oppressors and freed the country from Hellenistic control. This was followed by two revolts against the Romans (or three, if one counts the revolt of Egyptian Jews against the Romans). The end of the Roman wars was punctuated by the fall of the bastion at Masada, where the last 1,000 defenders committed suicide rather than surrender and live as slaves under Roman rule.

In modern times, the Jews of the Warsaw Ghetto rebelled against the Germans for a period of one month. The revolt began on the first day of Passover,

April 19, 1943, and effectively ended on May 18, 1943. This revolt presaged revolts in other Ghettos at Bialystok and Minsk, as well as in the killing centers and concentration camps of Sobibor and Treblinka. Finally, when the State of Israel was created in May of 1948, the grand plan of the attackers was to destroy the fledgling Jewish state; the Israelis won. These patterns of military defense were a direct reflection of the action of self-defense of Moses/Akhenaten and his military contingents.

H. Identification with the Land

Perhaps most important to Moses/Akhenaten's creation of an ethnic identification for the people of the Exodus was the issue of creating a homeland. As earlier stated, the right of the Egyptian sovereign to rule the land was based upon a gift of the land by the gods to the pharaoh. We have seen that, when Tutankhamun changed his theological affiliation from Aten to Amun, he was accepted by the priests of Amun. This disconnected Akhenaten from being the ruler of the *land* of Egypt and effectively ended his reign. Tutankhamun then became the ruler, because *he* was then tied to the *land*. When Horemheb died, Akhenaten, being the last survivor of the Eighteenth Dynasty, attempted to regain the throne. As we have seen, he was unsuccessful and, after leaving the land of Egypt, neither Moses/ Akhenaten nor the Hebrew people had a land to call their own. This crisis required immediate resolution, because Moses/Akhenaten desperately sought to ensure the viability of his theology.

Moses/Akhenaten found the answer in a vestigial relationship of the Hebrews with the land of Canaan. This relationship reflected two things: 1) There was, even then, a prior historical connection between the Hebrews and the land of Canaan; and 2) there appear to have been Hebrews still living in Canaan who had not descended to Egypt. This allowed Moses/Akhenaten to promulgate and reinforce the belief that the Hebrews had been promised the land of Canaan by God. Further, *if they had a land of their own*, they would survive as one nation and the ethical monotheism of Moses/Akhenaten would survive as the raison d'être of the people.

Today, it is easy for people to look at the seemingly endless and intractable claims, from both Jews and Muslims, over sovereignty of the land of Israel and sarcastically ask: "Since when is God a real estate agent?" It is difficult to properly respond to this question. It is insufficient for a Jew to state, in the words of the "Exodus" song by Andy Williams, that "This land is mine; God gave this land to me; this brave and ancient land to me." That expression of identification and dedication to the land is also raised by many Palestinian Muslims, whether as citizens of the modern state of Israel, as residents of the West Bank, or otherwise. In fact, many Muslims in areas of Israel, Gaza and the West Bank recognize that, in the distant or not-too-distant past, they had *Jewish* ancestry. They gave up their identification as Jews, but not their identification to the land; the land was paramount to them in their living patterns.

The best response from Jews regarding the right of sovereignty begins with and continues from actions of Moses/Akhenaten as set forth in the Torah: 1) The ancient Hebrews mentally and emotionally identified with the land of Israel; 2) they proceeded to inhabit the land; 3) they purchased parts of the land and, as a matter of contract law, owned it; 4) they maintained identification with the land as a cardinal provision of their religious faith for more than 3,000 years; 5) they always shared the land with non-Jews; 6) in modern times, they restored the land by draining the swamps in Galilee and eradicating malaria; 7) they irrigated the land to make it productive; 8) they reforested the land to give the land new life; and 9) they created a vibrant pluralistic society to live in the land. In other words, while Jews love the land equally as do the Palestinian Muslims, the Jews have *earned*, and by their actions *continue to earn*, the right to live in at least part of the traditional homeland.

When, in 1948, Jews were permitted by the United Nations to claim the land of Israel as their sovereign state, the Jews agreed to a partition of the "homeland" so that both Jews and non-Jews (Muslims, Christians and Druze) could live in close proximity and in the general biblical area of the ancient Jewish Kingdom. Then, in 1967, when the Israel Defense Forces regained sovereignty over the entire city of Jerusalem, they *did not dispossess* the non-Jews; in fact, the Grand Mufti was left in charge of the Temple Mount. The Jerusalem Islamic Waqf is an Islamic trust best known for controlling and managing Islamic edifices on the Al-Aqsa Mosque and Dome of the Rock sites in Jerusalem. The Waqf has governed access to the Temple Mount region since the Muslim reconquest of the Crusader Kingdom of Jerusalem in 1187. The Waqf consists of a director, the Grand Mufti of Jerusalem and the Islamic Council. Israel allowed the Waqf to retain its authority over the Temple Mount after Israel's liberation of Jerusalem as a result of the Six-Day War in 1967.

Non-Jews of Israel (whether Christian, Muslim, Druze, or otherwise) are accorded Israeli citizenship, are eligible to be elected to governmental office and can serve in the Knesset. In any event, the actions of biblical and modern-day Jews have always been directed to elevate the land and all of its inhabitants to productivity and grandeur.

VI. Priesthood, Temple Sacrifices and Relationship of Individuals to God

Moses/Akhenaten provided a framework for religious leadership in his struggle to make his new religion viable. He also was required to establish a relationship between the individual Hebrews and God.

A. Priests and Temple Sacrifices

Before his exile, Moses/Akhenaten had taken the position that he was the sole high priest to serve and communicate with the Aten. When he went into exile, he led a priesthood consisting of Levites. Meryare II (Aaron) was the preeminent priest of Akhetaten and Panhesy (Phineas) was the chief servitor of Atenism. When the exile(s) to Sinai occurred, there apparently was a raging conflict between Moses/Akhenaten, on the one hand, and Aaron and Phineas on the other. Aaron became the acknowledged first high priest; later Phineas (Pinchas) was appointed as the (subsequent) high priest. Moses/Akhenaten relinquished, or was required to relinquish, his claim to being the high priest. The Talmud discusses this action of relinquishment:

> The Rabbis tell us that Moses was not reluctant to accept this mission [of leading the Hebrews from Egypt] but ... he thought it should rightly belong to Aaron, his elder brother. Yet God was displeased with Moses, and, therefore, He gave the priesthood which He had designed for him, to Aaron, in saying: "Is there not Aaron thy brother, the Levite?"
>
> When God said "thy brother," the word "Levite" was implied, because Moses being a Levite, his brother must necessarily have been the same; but this was God's meaning: "I thought to make thee my priest, and continue thy brother, the Levite; but for thy reluctance in obeying my wishes, he shall be the priest and thou the Levite."[11]

Osman reflects this same distinction:

> Where Akhenaten, as we shall see, looked upon himself as the high priest of his God, the Talmud tells us that "Moses officiated as the high priest. He was also considered the King of Israel during the sojourn in the desert." Where did the rabbis obtain the facts in the Talmud? They can hardly have invented them and, indeed, had no reason to do so. ... The Talmudic stories contain many distortions and accretions arising from the fact that they were transmitted orally for a long time before finally being set down in writing. Yet one can sense that behind the myths there must have lain genuine historical events that had been suppressed from the official accounts of both Egypt and Israel, but had survived in the memories of the generations.[12]

In contrast, at the end of Deuteronomy 34:10, the text states: "And there hath not risen a prophet since in Israel like unto Moses, whom the Lord knew face to face." Deuteronomy *redefines* the position of Moses from being a high priest to being the greatest prophet or leader.

It would appear that Moses/Akhenaten struggled mightily against Aaron and Pinchas (Phineas) for definition and supremacy of their respective positions. Moses/Akhenaten appears to have resolved this struggle by surrendering any claim to being the high priest of God in exchange for the support of the Levites as their leader. Reciprocally, the Levites were apparently required to similarly surrender, with respect to the Hebrew body politic, any claim to being the sole priests, in the sense of being intermediaries, to and with God. The result of that struggle was that *each individual* Hebrew had a *direct relationship with God*.

In any event, before Moses/Akhenaten, the Hebrews had no priesthood or hierarchy of priests. After Moses/Akhenaten, there was a definitive structuring, so that the descendants of Aaron and, later, of Pinchas became the high priests (Cohanim), the remaining Levites were their assistants (Leviyim) and the balance of the Hebrews became the body politic of Israel ("Yisroel"). (This tension between Moses and Aaron and their descendants appears to have continued for hundreds of years and seems to explain why the descendants of Moses apparently settled in the north of the promised land, being the Kingdom of Israel, and the descendants of Aaron settled in the south, being the Kingdom of Judea). Tracy R. Rich notes the following. In Judaism, a priest is:

> charged with performing various rites in the *Temple* in connection with religious rituals and *sacrifices*. ... Since the destruction of the *Temple* ... rabbis have taken over the spiritual leadership of the Jewish community. ... However, it is important to note that the rabbi's status as rabbi does not give him any special authority to conduct religious services. Any Jew sufficiently educated to know what he is doing can lead a religious service.[13]

Before leaving this subject, we should consider the issue of sacrifice. Much of the Book of Leviticus deals with sacrifices. However, because there is no sacrificial practice in Judaism today, and *never* again will be an active part of Judaism, no further reference is made in this book to the subject of sacrifices.

B. Relationship between God and the Individual

As noted above, in Judaism priests are not intermediaries between God and the individual. Each person has an individual right and prerogative to directly address or petition to God. This probably stems from Exodus 19:6 which states: "and ye shall be unto Me a kingdom of priests." Hertz, editor of one of the main Torah and Haftorah commentaries, amplifies by stating that this text connotes "a kingdom whose citizens are all priests."[14]

There is an interesting portion of the Book of the Prophets, which is read (as a Haftorah portion) on the first day of Rosh Hashanah. (A Haftorah is a reading, supplemental to a Torah reading, from the Prophets or the Writings.) This Haftorah, from I Samuel, sets forth an interesting commentary on, and illustrates the principle of, the individual relationship to God. In this Haftorah, Elkanah is stated to be married to Hannah. Hannah is barren of child. Hannah desperately wants to bear a son. The verses are as follows:

v 9   Now Eli the priest sat upon his seat by the door-post of the temple of the Lord;

v 10   and she [Hannah] was in bitterness of soul-and prayed unto the Lord, and wept sore...

v 12   And it came to pass, as she prayed long before the Lord, that Eli watched her mouth.

v 13 Now Hannah, she spoke in her heart; only her lips moved, but her voice could not be heard; therefore Eli thought she had been drunken.

v 14 And Eli said unto her: 'How long wilt thou be drunken? Put away thy wine from thee.'

v 15 And Hannah answered and said: 'No, my lord, I am a woman of a sorrowful spirit; I have drunk neither wine nor strong drink, but I poured out my soul before the Lord.

v 16 'Count not thy handmaid for a wicked woman; for out of the abundance of my complaint and my vexation have I spoken hitherto.'

v 17 Then Eli answered and said: 'Go in peace, and the God of Israel grant thy petition that thou hast asked of Him.'

From the prayer of Hannah, we vividly see the *direct* relationship between an individual and God which exists in Judaism.[k] As noted previously, neither Moses nor the Levites had, or were able to maintain, a role as an intermediary in that relationship.

VII. Vestments, Music and Instruments

In addition to the priestly structure, the Torah sets forth detailed references to vestments, pageantry, musical instruments and song; these were transferred and modified for the Hebrews by the Levites, when changing from their role as priests to and for Atenism to their role as priests for the new religion of the Hebrews. As a simple example, vestments of both the Levites and of the earlier Atenist priests were required to be of linen.

Perhaps more interesting is the usage, and apparent evolution, of the pharaonic headdress. There were several royal crowns. We will consider only the khepresh. It was blue and made of cloth. It was covered with yellow sun discs, representing the sun god Aten. Like many other royal crowns, a serpent (uraeus) was fastened to its front. Amenhotep III, the father of Akhenaten/Moses, was apparently the first pharaoh to be depicted wearing the blue crown. Akhenaten/Moses wore the khepresh, as is depicted in Appendix I, figure 3. There are at least two statues of Akhenaten/Moses showing him wearing the khepresh.

Apparently, some of the members of the Egyptian priesthood wore crowns. But, more interestingly, in ancient Israel the Kohen Gadol (High Priest) wore a headdress which was wound around his head to form a broad, flat-topped cloth turban. This was called a mitznefet. Unlike a khepresh, with sun discs and an uraeus, a tzitz was attached to the mitznefet by straps. The tzitz was a golden breastplate bearing the inscription "Holiness to YMWH." The word tzitz appears

---

k   It is evident that silent prayer was not common place at that time. That reference, therefore, indicates that the silent prayer, the Amidah, was patterned after the silent prayer of Hannah.

to be related to the word tzitzit, which denotes the fringes required in the Torah to be attached to clothing or, later, the fringes attached to a religious shawl, called a tallit. In ancient times, the tzitzit was required to contain a thread of *blue* (as in the color of the khepresh). [15]

Not everyone could wear a gold breastplate (tzitz) because it was cumbersome, but anyone wearing a tzitzit wore a strand of blue. As is explained above dealing with the relationship of the individual to God, each Hebrew was a member of a kingdom whose every citizen was a priest of God. Therefore, if blue were a sign of holiness, each person would appropriately be connected to God by wearing the blue tzitzit.

There are, therefore, several apparent relationships between the khepresh, the mitznefet and the blue tzitzit:

A.   The khepresh and mitznefet were both cloth head coverings;

B.   Both head coverings made reference to the single God;

C.   The headdresses were worn by royalty or by the priesthood to display authority.

D.   The khepresh with its yellow sun discs appears to have evolved to the mitznefet with its attached tzitz and, in turn, to have then evolved from the mitznefet to the more portable tzitzit. More succinctly, there appears to have been an evolving relationship between the khepresh and the tzitzit. The *blue* crown khepresh of a pharaoh appears to have evolved into the required blue thread of a tallit.

There is one additional relationship. Now that there is no longer a Kohen Gadol (High Priest) to wear a mitznefet, the head covering of the Jewish people is generally more modest in size. The Hebrew term for the current head covering of the Jewish people is a kippah. The word *khepresh* may be the etymological antecedent of the word *kippah*.

The thrust of this section is *not* that there were commonalities between the vestments, music and instruments of the Egyptians and of the Hebrews. The significance is that, despite the great civilization and accomplishments of the Egyptians, the civilization of the ancient Egyptians and their accomplishments have ceased to have any current viability, other than as archeological artifacts and matters of historical curiosity and interest. Conversely, as a result of the efforts of Moses/Akhenaten and his Levite companions, the Egyptian civilization and its practice morphed, and became integrated, into the continuing living culture and religion of Judaism begun by Moses/Akhenaten and his Levite companions.

VIII.   Physical Structure

Moses/Akhenaten provided a physical structure and edifice for the Hebrews' place of worship. He defined the requirements of the tent and/or Tabernacle used

63

in the Sinai which, as Friedman demonstrates, became "sized" to the dimensions that were later used in the Holy of Holies in the First Great Temple, erected by King Solomon.[16]

Moses/Akhenaten also mandated the placement and positioning of the structure of the house of worship. First, in the city of Akhetaten, Akhenaten/Moses caused the temple of Aten to face the east (to relate to the rising of the sun god, Aten). Jewish tradition reflects that Moses, too, caused the Tabernacle to face the east. The text of Numbers 3:38 is: "And those that were to pitch before the tabernacle eastward, before the tent of meeting toward the sunrising, were Moses, and Aaron and his sons." Note also that Numbers 25:4 describes a scene where God tells Moses to take idolaters out to face into the sun [i.e. to face the east]. This placement toward the east has continued to this day, although the rationale is now that the placement is toward Jerusalem rather than to the sun.

Second, the Egyptian Holy of Holies contained holy relics; in the case of Amenhotep III, the pharaoh lodged the royal barge, "Aten Gleams," in the Holy of Holies. Moses/Akhenaten changed this so that the Holy of Holies was to contain a box-like ark, which itself was to contain the tablets of the Ten Commandments. After the destruction of the first temple, the Ark of the Covenant (and the tablets of the Ten Commandments) disappeared and the Holy of Holies remained empty; the Holy of Holies then became fully reflective of the abstract nature of the monotheism of Moses/Akhenaten.

At this juncture, we should consider the similarities and differences between the holy relics contained in the Holy of Holies of the Egyptian temples and of the Holy of Holies contained in the temples of Moses/Akhenaten (and in the tent or tabernacle used in the Sinai). In the Egyptian temple at the time of Amenhotep III (the father of Akhenaten/Moses), the relic was the boat, Aten Gleams. In this regard "gleams" relates to the radiant light emanating from Aten (being the sun god). In the Holy of Holies of Moses/Akhenaten, the holy object was the Ark of the Covenant (and the tablets of the Ten Commandments). In each case, the contents of the Holy of Holies related to the glory of God. However, in the Egyptian temple, the holy object connected god solely to the pharaoh and his queen. In contrast, in the Hebrew temple, the holy object related to a connection between God and *each* individual member of the congregation and, accordingly, each member of the Hebrew congregation was directly and *individually* connected to God through the contents of (or, later, in the lack of contents in) the Holy of Holies.

IX. Writing and Education

Akhenaten and his Levite priests had inherited a written form of Egyptian inscription called hieroglyphics. However, early in his reign, Akhenaten and his Levite priests had learned, or developed, the art of writing with letters of an alphabet. Therefore, while Moses/Akhenaten had been fluent in the Egyptian language,

Moses/Akhenaten might have been able, through the help of Aaron and the Levitical priesthood, to reduce the Hebrew language into an alphabetical script. In this regard, the Tablets of the Ten Commandments could have been inscribed in either Hebrew or Egyptian. The fact that it took a long time, reportedly forty days, to chisel inscriptions into stone tablets would reflect the physical difficulty of stone carving and slowness engendered by an early and unfamiliar usage of alphabetical characters, whether in Egyptian or Hebrew.

In this regard, a report by Clara Moskowitz, staff writer for Livescience.com, states that:

> Scientists have discovered the earliest known Hebrew writing — an inscription dating from the 10th century B.C., [comes from] ... the period of King David's reign.
>
> The breakthrough could mean that portions of the Bible were written centuries earlier than previously thought. (The Bible's Old Testament is thought to have been first written down in an ancient form of Hebrew.)
>
> Until now, many scholars have held that the Hebrew Bible originated in the 6th century B.C., because Hebrew writing was thought to stretch back no further. But the newly deciphered Hebrew text is about four centuries older, scientists announced this month.
>
> 'It indicates that the Kingdom of Israel already existed in the 10th century B.C. and that at least some of the biblical texts were written hundreds of years before the dates presented in current research,' said Gershon Galil, a professor of Biblical Studies at the University of Haifa in Israel, who deciphered the ancient text.[17]

It is, therefore, possible that an even earlier use of Hebrew letters, such as in the tablets of the Ten Commandments, also occurred. However, even if the inscriptions were not made in Hebrew, the use of any written script for purposes of Hebrew theology and liturgy represented a quantum leap in religious practice.

It is often said that Jews are the "People of the Book." Moses/Akhenaten began to establish, as we will see below, Jewish liturgy and religious practices. But because of the direct relationship of each individual with God, it became incumbent upon Jews to become familiar with the written texts of the Torah, Tanakh and other later writings. Familiarity required literacy, hence the "People of the Book." The teachings of Moses/Akhenaten and the Levites required questioning and intellectual reasoning. This pattern continues to this very day.

X. Liturgy

Moses/Akhenaten created the beginnings of Jewish liturgy. Moses/Akhenaten was a dreamer and a poet as well. This is evidenced in his Hymn to the Aten.

A. Hymn to the Aten and the Psalm of David (Psalm 104)

The substance of the words of the Hymn to the Aten are the following:

> The cattle are content in their pasture, the trees and plants are green, the birds fly from their nests. Their wings are raised in praise of your soul. The goats leap on their feet. All flying and fluttering things live when you shine for them. Likewise the boats race up and down the river, and every way is open, because you have appeared. The fish in the river leap before your face. Your rays go to the depth of the sea.[18]

The Psalm of David (Psalm 104) parallels the content and imagery of the Hymn to the Aten. It is substantially the following:

> He causeth the grass to grow for the cattle, and the herb for the service of man: that he may bring forth food out of the earth: and wine that maketh glad the heart of man and oil to make his face shine, and bread which strengtheneth man's heart. The trees of the Lord are full of sap: the cedars of Lebanon which he hath planted: where the birds make their nests: as for the stork, the fir trees are her house. The high hills are a refuge for the wild goats; and the rocks for the conies. ... So is this great and wide sea, wherein are things creeping innumerable, both great and small beasts. There go the ships.

The similarity of the sequence and images in both compositions is striking. As such, many believe that the earlier Egyptian hymn must have been known to the later Hebrew writer.

The continuing use of great amounts of poetry in Jewish liturgy is manifested today in current prayer books.

B. Source of Daily Prayers Referencing Celestial Bodies

I believe that the daily prayers in current Jewish liturgy, beginning with the "Barachu" and ending with the "Shema," relate, in substance if not in exact form, with the liturgical innovations of Moses/Akhenaten. These prayers include many references to light and to celestial bodies, such as the sun. They are unique in the liturgy. These specific prayers may or may not have been written by Moses/Akhenaten or the Levites, but the imagery and subject matter appear to relate back to Moses/Akhenaten. This is the point at which the possible derivation of Aaron's (Hebrew) name from the Egyptian language is relevant. That translation of "Aaron" means "bringer of light."

C. Song of the Sea

As noted in Chapter Six, Jewish tradition posits that Moses/Akhenaten wrote a song of praise, the Song of the Sea, to God upon the defeat and drowning of the pursuing Egyptian host. Miriam/Nefertiti also wrote a Song of the Sea. We will further expand upon these texts and the relationship of Moses/Akhenaten to

Miriam/Nefertiti regarding these texts in Chapter Eight pertaining to Miriam/Nefertiti.

D. Passover

While not set forth in the texts as a specific prayer, Exodus 12 establishes the institution of the Passover holiday and celebration. This necessarily resulted in development of liturgy to commemorate the Passover season. This liturgy was later reduced to writing in the Haggadah. The customs and ceremonies set forth in the Haggadah, including, most importantly, the use of Matzah and the contents of the Seder plate, are representative of this religious development.

E. Shema

Most important is the construction and interpretation of the Shema. This is the credo of the Jewish religion. It is very succinct:

Shema Yisrael Adonai Elohenu Adonai Echod.

Hear O Israel the Lord Our God, The Lord is One.

Osman paraphrases Sigmund Freud in showing that the Hebrew letter "d" is a transliteration of the Egyptian letter "t" and that "o" is a transliteration of the Egyptian letter "e." Osman further points out that:

The Hebrew word "Adonai" is also usually rendered in English as "Lord." …

The "ai" can be removed from the word "Adonai" as it is a Hebrew pronoun meaning "my" or "mine" and signifying possession. We are then left with "Adon" (Lord) which, as correctly noted by Freud, is the Hebrew word for the Egyptian "Aten" as the Egyptian "t" becomes "d" in Hebrew and the vowel "e" becomes an "o." The name of the God of Moses, Adon, is therefore in the above references the same as the name of the God of Akhenaten, Aten. …

The question of God's name, however, seems to have been a matter of compromise. …

It seems that Akhenaten would not reject the name of his God, the Aten, simply to secure the support of the Israelites. Therefore a compromise had to be reached. Its nature was that, while the Hebrew word "YHWH" could be written, it could not be read aloud but had to be pronounced as "Adonai." Nobody knows when this Jewish practice started although I believe it dates from the time of Moses. Nor has any convincing explanation ever been put forward for the interdict. To say that a ban on uttering God's personal name was intended as a sign of respect is contradicted by the fact that all the other names given to the Israelite God before the time of Moses, as well as Adonai, are spoken aloud by the Jews. …

[It appears] that a compromise was reached in Sinai under which the old personal name of God, Jehovah, before the time of Moses would never be pronounced again and should in every case be replaced by Adonai, the name of the God of Akhenaten.[19]

Therefore, the sentence from the Shema could, as suggested by Freud and Osman, be translated: "Hear, O Israel, our God Aten is the Only God."

However, I would expand upon the analysis of Osman. Through an examination of Chapters 3 and 4 of Exodus, as further reflected in Appendix VIII, one can discern that there was an argument and compromise about usage of the theonym (i.e., substituted name of God). In these verses there is an inconsistent reflection of the name(s) of, or attributed to, God. Five terms for God are used in these two chapters; they are YHWH, Elohay, Elohim, Adonai and Eheyeh, which is a variable form of YHWH. There are also two combination forms of those words and a very strange of combination of two of those terms. Further complicating the matter of analyzing the text is that there are no vowels in the Torah, so the word "Adonai" may also be read as "Adoni." We should note the actual verbiage of some of the passages in the Torah, such as Exodus 4:10 and 13:

v10. And Moses said unto the Lord [YHWH]: "Oh, *Lord*, I am not a man of words … for I am slow of speech and of a slow tongue. …

v13. Oh, *Lord*, send [or identify the name of the person], I pray thee, … who thou wilt send …"

v14. and [God] said: "is there not Aaron, thy brother, the Levite? I know that he can speak well."

What is significant about verses 10 and 13 is that the Hebrew word for *Lord*, as expressed in the quotation of the spoken words of Moses/Akhenaten, is not written as YHWH, which is read and pronounced as the theonym Adonai, but the word *Lord* is written with the actual letters and spelling of the Hebrew word Adonai or Adoni. Therefore, the direct translation of verses 10 and 13, *uttered* by Moses/Akhenaten, is: "Oh, my Aten, I am not a man of words …" and "Oh, my Aten, send I pray thee …"

This does not diminish or belittle the Hebrew (Jewish) theology of the single God; it merely shows a progression in historic verbalizations of the name of, and for, God. At the time of expression of these verses, Moses/Akhenaten was on the verge of returning to Egypt for the last time and then leaving, as an Exodus, in the company of the mixed multitude which would become the people of Israel. His expression of the Egyptian name Aten in these verses reflected the progression in his thinking and in theological development. These verses, therefore, do *not* detract from the strength of Jewish theology; rather, they illuminate the evolution of those concepts, from the actual words of Moses/Akhenaten to the later writing of those words in the text of the Torah.

In any event, Exodus 3:13-14 introduces the substitution of Adonai for YHWH as follows:

And Moses said unto God: "Behold when I come unto the children of Israel, and shall say unto them: The God of your fathers hath sent me unto you; and they shall say to me, What is his name? What shall I say unto them?"

And God said unto Moses, "I AM THAT I AM." And He said, "Thus shalt thou say unto the children of Israel, I AM [YHWH] hath sent me unto you."

The text that states that the name of God is "I am that I am" is a *tour de force*, wherein the writers of the written Torah have cleverly modified the substitution of "Adonai" for YHWH/Jehovah by suggesting, and in fact stating, that the abstract nature of God is non-corporeal and is an integral part of the ethical structuring of monotheism. Thus, YHWH, which became "Adonai," then reverts to YHWH.

I would further expand upon Osman's analysis. To Osman and Freud, the key words in the Shema are those relating to the substitution of YHWH with Adonai. I submit that, for Jews, the key words are different; they are: "Hear," "Israel" and "One." I will address those three words in reverse order.

1) "One." All monotheistic religions face a common problem. If there is only one God and that one God is omniscient and omnipotent, then how does one explain the existence of evil? A merciful and loving God cannot be considered to be the creator of, or responsible for, evil. In other words, the concept of One God is a negative if one posits that the sole God is the creator of evil as well as of good or, alternatively, is uninterested in the travails of mankind. In that sense, the polytheistic rationale of multiple gods becomes easier to accept. "If there is one god, then two or more would be better." In other words, one god would explain nobility, decency and goodness and, conversely, evil would be explained by a separate god. In common parlance, many Christians explain evil as being separate from God, but being the handiwork of "Satan." Another rationale is that people refer to God as being the omnipotent creator of goodness, while tragedies, destruction and devastation, relating to disease and natural disasters, are the "hand of mother nature." I think that this conundrum is best solved by a point missed by Osman (and Freud). In Hebrew, the word "echad" means the numerical word "one," but, more importantly, it also means "singular" or "unique." (A similar identification exists in Latin, where the word "uno" means the numerical word "one', but the word uno is also the stem for the word unique.)

The essence of ethical monotheism is this uniqueness or singularity. God, or the conception of God in Judaism, requires the concept that Jews, and in fact non-Jews, are partners with God in the never-ending unfolding of history. As partners, God gives humankind life and opportunity; God assigns to humankind, as God's partner, responsibility for efforts and actions to suppress evil and nurture goodness.

2) "Israel." Jonathan Sacks, Chief Rabbi of the United Hebrew Congregation of the Commonwealth, ties the concept of singularity and uniqueness to the people of Israel by stating:

The faith of Israel declares the oneness of God and the plurality of man. This declaration constitutes ... universal solutions to the human situation. ... [The] conceptual structure of Judaism, with its belief in one God and many faiths, is as near as we have yet come to a world view that does justice to diversity while at the same time acknowledging the universal human condition. ... Judaism advances the daring idea that man and God are partners in the work of creation. Faith is the call to human responsibility. ...

Above all — and this has been my central theme — Judaism is not a theory, a system, a set of speculative propositions, an 'ism.' It is a call, and it bears our name. Unlike the other great monotheisms, Christianity and Islam, and equally unlike the philosophies of the Greeks and their successors, Judaism is not a truth addressed to all mankind. It is a summons to us, mediated through more than a hundred generations of our ancestors, written in the history of their lives and now confronting us as our heritage and responsibility. One of the most profound religious truths Judaism ever articulated was that God loves diversity; He does not ask us all to serve Him in the same way. To each people He has set a challenge, and with the Jewish people He made a covenant, knowing that it takes time, centuries, millennia, to overcome the conflicts and injustices of the human situation, and that therefore each generation must hand on its ideals to the next, so that there will always be a Jewish people conveying its particular vision to humanity and moving, however haltingly, to a more gracious world. The most eloquent words God spoke to Abraham, Jacob, Moses and the prophets was to call their name. The reply was simply *Hineni*, 'Here I am.' That is the call Jewish history makes to us: to continue the story and to write our letter in the scroll.[20]

The foregoing observation of Rabbi Sachs hints at the tension between Judaism and the philosophies of Hellenism. More importantly, it eloquently sets forth the concept of being the "Chosen People." Jews are not better than anyone else; to the contrary, Jews have adopted, as part of their ethos, a positive undertaking to act throughout their lives with goodness, and also an undertaking to be accepting of the diversity of others and accepting of the contributions of others to goodness and godliness. In that effort to act with goodness, Jews and Judaism act as the conscience of mankind.

We are required to do good. To the extent of our success, we are likened to the divine. To the extent of our failure, we are required to do better. This is the only way that the evils of the Holocaust, genocide of any people, deaths of innocents or any other heart-wrenching situation can be reconciled. I believe that the concept of being the Chosen People, set forth in the Torah to be that of a covenant between the people of Israel and God, derives directly from the theology of Moses/Akhenaten and the compromises made between Moses/Akhenaten with Aaron/Meryare II, Pinchas and the Levites.

Therefore, the Shema should be interpreted as:

"Hear O Israel, the Lord our God, the Lord is one."

Or, better:

"Hear O Israel, the Lord our God, the Lord is *unique.*"

3) "Hear." When Moses and Aaron reached the accommodation of referring to God (YHWH) as Adonai, part of the compromise was to add the word "Hear." The expression is *not* "O Israel, the Lord our God, the Lord is One and Unique." Rather, there is a *mandate* given by the initial word of the Shema: *Hear,* meaning *Listen Up!* A Jew is required to not merely passively acknowledge the uniqueness and singularity of God, but a Jew must act upon that acknowledgment as a personal mandate.

XI. Free Will

Judaism champions the concept of free will. This is addressed in Deuteronomy 30:19:

"I call heaven and earth to witness against you this day that I have set before thee life and death … therefore choose life, that those mayest live."

Hertz, in a footnote to that verse, comments that the term "choose life" means "exercise free will." Jewish ethics is rooted in the doctrine of human responsibility, being *freedom of the will.*[21]

This concept of free will is exemplified by the following:

A. The requirement of doing good is its own reward;

B. The mandate of the Ten Commandments can only be accomplished through exercise of free will;

C. Charity is a result of choice.

D. Freedom which is directed to a good purpose is a result of choice.

E. Fair treatment of women and non-Jews is a result of choice.

F. Help given to others during events of human crisis and natural disasters is a demonstration of free will.

G. Israeli and Jewish reverence for the land of Israel is an exercise of choice.

XII. Commencement

The word commencement often indicates an end, as in a graduation (commencement) ceremony. However, the strict meaning of that word is a beginning. The word commencement therefore uniquely applies to the subject matter of this chapter.

Moses/Akhenaten, Miriam/Nefertiti and the Levites created a complex religious structure.

It has been said that Judaism has three aspects: 1) a theology of ethical monotheism; 2) a cultural paradigm; and 3) a nationalistic identification tied to the specific land of Israel. Moses/Akhenaten and the Levites were, effectively, brilliant in their ability to create such a tripartite theological, cultural and national framework.

Moses/Akhenaten could not have predicted the destruction of the kingdom of Judea and the resulting exile of Jews at the end of the last of the Jewish-Roman wars. The destruction of the Judean state required a redefinition of Judaism by the rabbis of Yavneh. The rabbis substituted the emphasis and focal point of sacrificial services and offerings in the Great Temple with the requirement to study Torah. Further, Moses/Akhenaten could not have predicted the systematic genocidal program instituted by Hitler during the Holocaust. The antidote for Nazism and the Holocaust was the creation of the State of Israel, which then became a place of refuge for any Jews of the Diaspora threatened with persecution and oppression. What is significant about the tripartite framework of theology, culture and national identity to the land is that these three components of Judaism provided a basis for the very survival of Judaism in the face of such recurring disasters.

So the *end* of the efforts of Moses/Akhenaten, being the creation of a new religion, was merely the *beginning* of a continuing historical evolution of Judaism and the continuing partnership of Jews and non-Jews with God.

8

MIRIAM/NEFERTITI & AARON/MERYARE II

While it seems reasonably easy to cross-identify Akhenaten and Moses, it is not quite as easy to cross-identify other biblical characters. The Torah identifies Aaron as the brother of Moses. It states that he is a Levite. Ultimately, he is appointed as high priest. Similarly, Meryare II was the high priest in the Temple of Aten. As we have noted, one of the meanings of the name Aaron in Egyptian is "bringer of light," and the meaning of Meryare in Egyptian is "beloved." Both names in the Egyptian language effectively relate to a position of royalty or, in this context, of priesthood.

We have noted that Moses and the Levites struggled for positions of authority in the exile. This is particularly evident in the foregoing discussion of the credo of Judaism, the Shema. While Aaron/Meryare II generally took a subservient role to Moses/Akhenaten, several stories in the Torah relate the power struggle between them, including the story of the golden calf (which was built under the oversight of Aaron while Moses was receiving the Ten Commandments), the story of the Cushite wife (discussed below), and the stories of the biblical writers J and E on the one hand, and P on the other, in their references to Moses and Aaron. P normally wrote of Moses *and Aaron*: "and God spoke to Moses *and Aaron*" (emphasis added). When J and E wrote of Moses (and Aaron), they emphasized Moses: "and God spoke to Moses."[1]

Perhaps more importantly, on at least one occasion, Aaron speaks to Moses as a subject would speak to his king. This appears in Numbers 12:11: "and Aaron said unto Moses: 'Oh my lord. ...'" In this line, Aaron uses the word Adoni. Because there are no vowels in the Torah text, Adoni is spelled identically to the word Adonai. However, it is clear that Aaron is referring to Moses/Akhenaten as a monarch (i.e. pharaoh) and not as a divine being. Equally remarkable, in the preceding chapter of the Torah, Numbers 11:28, Joshua uses this same term, lord or Adoni, as an acknowledgment of a kingly (i.e. pharaonic) status of Moses/Akhenaten: "and Joshua ... said: 'my lord Moses ...'"

Pinchas is subsequently appointed as high priest in Numbers 25:13. It is noteworthy that the Hebrew name "Pinchas" is the corollary to "Panhesy," who was the chief servitor of the Aten at the temple in Akhetaten. Pinchas, however, does not show the same degree of subservience to Moses/Akhenaten as does Aaron/Meryare II. We see this in Numbers 25:7-8, where Pinchas takes a spear in his hand, follows two sinning Israelites into the tent and "thrusts both of them through, the man of Israel and the woman through her belly." While the action of Pinchas is very dramatic and the text shows that God rewarded him with the status of being the next High Priest of Israel, his action is very definitely a violation of the Sixth Commandment: thou shalt not murder. Pinchas, rather than showing humility, shows an increasingly hostile and aggressive pattern of conduct. From his passive allegiance to Akhenaten/Moses in city of Akhetaten, he has become a man, at times, of extreme aggression.

It is also not as easy to cross identify Miriam and Nefertiti as it is Akhenaten and Moses.[1] It should be noted that the root-stem for beloved, "Mry," which is common to both Aaron/Meryare II and Miriam/Nefertiti, connotes an expression of royalty. As previously noted, in English this would be similar to addressing the Queen (or King) of England with the phrase: "Your Royal Highness" (or "Your Majesty").

In both life stories, Miriam/Nefertiti is said to be the older sister of Moses/Akhenaten and has a strong relationship with him. However, Nefertiti disappears suddenly from Egyptian history in approximately the fourteenth year of Akhenaten's reign. Yet, there is evidence of her continued existence and residence in the city of Akhetaten after that time. Similarly, Miriam dies/disappears abruptly in Exodus 10:1: "Miriam died there, and was buried there." End of story. While the stories of Miriam and Nefertiti are not identical, it is significant that both stories end so very abruptly.

Perhaps the strongest evidence that Miriam/Nefertiti were the same person is

---

1   The Torah speaks of Moses' wife being Zipporah. Osman and Pope make convincing arguments that "Zipporah" is merely a pseudonym for Queen Tiye.

found in Numbers 12:1-3, 13:

v 1   And Miriam and Aaron spoke against Moses because of the Cushite woman whom he had married; for he had married a Cushite woman.

v 2   And they said: 'Hath the Lord indeed spoken only with Moses? Hath He not spoken also with us?' And the Lord heard it.

v 3   Now the man Moses was very meek, above all the men that were upon the face of the earth. ...

v 13 And Moses cried unto the Lord, saying: 'Heal her now, O God, I beseech Thee.'

Most commentators focus on the apparent carping of Miriam and Aaron, God's rejection of their complaining and the apparent punishment of Miriam. However, verse 3 seems to be strangely placed and not adequately analyzed. I will shortly deal with my interpretation of the significance of verse 3.

However, first we should identify the Cushite woman. Osman identifies the Cushite wife as being Queen Tiye.[2] The bust of Queen Tiye, seen in Appendix I, figure 6, indicates facial features consistent with an Ethiopian (i.e. Cushite) woman. The Talmud supports this identification when it relates that Moses, after fleeing from Egypt, had made his way to Ethiopia. He became a favorite of the old king and when the king died Moses was appointed as the new king. The widow of the deceased king became the wife of Moses. The widow is identified as Adonith, which is a variation of Aten-it, which is itself a derivative of the name of the sun god, Aten. The Talmud, in referring to the king's widow whom Moses marries as Aten-it, directly connects Queen Tiye to Moses. Osman points out that the Koran embellishes on, and reinforces, the Talmudic story.

It is well established that Akhenaten and Nefertiti were childhood sweethearts. Also, Nefertiti was more fully and frequently pictorially represented than Akhenaten, indicating that she was of royal rank. The Egyptian records support the conclusion that, because Akhenaten and Nefertiti bore six daughters and no sons, Akhenaten then married Queen Tiye, his mother, in order to sire a male heir. She was likely the mother of Tutankhamun.

Miriam/Nefertiti's terse statement about Moses/Akhenaten's Cushite wife could reflect the ire of Nefertiti/Miriam that he had displaced her in favor of her mother-in-law. Miriam/Nefertiti, who was the childhood love of Moses/Akhenaten, shows her anger by an implied question: "Moses how could you have done that?" Aaron apparently shared that anger because he also rejected the incestuous sexual relationship. Both Miriam/Nefertiti and Aaron/Meryare II also appeared to have been critical of Queen Tiye (the Cushite wife) because her motivation in rejecting Akhenaten/Moses (as set forth in the Talmud) was that she believed the dynasty would be better served by Tutankhamun, rather than Akhenaten/Moses. Apparently, Miriam/Nefertiti and Aaron/Meryare II bridled at the incestuous conduct of Moses/Akhenaten and the streak of total self-interest demonstrated by Queen Tiye. The result is that incest and incestuous marriage are strongly rejected in Leviticus 18: 6-21. (See Appendix VII.) The placement of 18:6-21 between the continuing stories of Moses (in Exodus and Numbers), seems to have been purposeful, so as to dramatically reject and disapprove of Moses/Akhenaten's incestuous relationships.

However, let us return to Numbers 12:3. This verse is often translated as, "Moses was very modest, above all men that were upon the face of the earth." The translation previously used in this chapter does not use the word "modest"; it uses the word "meek." How does that translation fit into the balance of the text? Again, I think the subtext of Numbers 12 is that Miriam and Aaron were angry because of the incestuous relationship of Moses/Akhenaten with Queen Tiye. Moses/Akhenaten reacted to their anger by being *contrite* (i.e., meek), because they had caused him to personally acknowledge his rejection of Nefertiti/Miriam, who was the love of his life. I think the true meaning of verse 3 is that Moses was effectively chastened by the rebukes of Miriam/Nefertiti and Aaron/Meryare II. Further, when Miriam/Nefertiti appears to have been punished by God, Moses/Akhenaten in verse 13, in a sign of total contrition, expresses one of the shortest prayers in the Torah: "Heal her now, O God, I beseech thee." This prayer is consistent with his seeking of forgiveness, whether from God or from Miriam/Nefertiti, for rejecting his sister/wife in favor of Queen Tiye, his mother.

It is further significant to review and analyze the Song of the Sea (included in its entirety in Appendix III). Robin Cohn, in Biblical Women Week by Week, discusses the involvement of Miriam the prophetess in crafting the Song of the Sea:

> The scattered references to Miriam throughout the Hebrew Bible leave us with the impression that her role was far greater than what has been handed down to us. From [other references] we learn that it would be presumptuous to think that nothing else was recorded about Miriam, including her prophetic utterances. ...
>
> Miriam performed a victory dance-song, a celebration honoring the returning warrior carried out exclusively by women. ... Most scholars have come to the conclusion that both the short and long versions of the song should be attributed to Miriam and therefore have renamed it, the Song of Miriam. "The accumulated weight of literary, textual, historical, sociological, musicological, and feminist research on Exodus 15 indicates that Miriam is the more likely author. Indeed, the fact that the Song is a victory hymn, a genre associated with female rather than male musicians, in itself is a compelling enough reason to assign composition to Miriam rather than to her more famous brother" (Meyers, Exodus, p.116).
>
> Recently a third theory has taken shape, namely that originally there existed a longer song attributed to Miriam, similar but not identical to the "Song of the Sea" which has traditionally [been] attributed to Moses. A fragment

found among the Dead Sea Scrolls … contains [seven] lines of poetic text just after Miriam's two-line song we are familiar with in the canon. The fragment reads:

1. you despised [or: you plundered] …
2. for the triumph of …
3. you are great, a savior …
4. the hope of the enemy perishes and he is …
5. they perished in the mighty waters, the enemy …
6. and he exalted her to their heights … you gave …
7. working a triumph.

What we learn here is that Miriam had her own song similar to but not the same as the 'Song of Moses.' Although this handful of fragmented lines of Miriam's song echoes portions of the unbroken song we have in the Hebrew Bible, it also 'signals other themes, including, in the phrase "and he exalted her to their heights," an indication that God acted to save his people in part through a woman, Miriam.' … Although it has been assumed that Miriam led only the women in song and Moses the men, the grammar of the songs tells us that both songs were addressed to all the people and the singers were not divided by gender.[3]

There are many commentaries on the Song of the Sea. An article by Dewayne Bryant, writing for Apologeticspress.org, contains some important insights:

On February 26, 2010, the *Associated Press* reported that two pieces of a biblical manuscript had been reunited after being separated for centuries. … The fragments date to the 7th century A.D., a period during which almost no Hebrew manuscripts survive. This exciting discovery has once again drawn the world's attention back, not only to one of the earliest books of the Hebrew Bible, but one of its earliest sections.

The two portions together contain the Song of the Sea from Exodus 15:1-20. The song was sung just after the crossing of the Red/Reed Sea (Exodus 14). The song celebrates God's victory over the Egyptian military, which was the strongest at the time in the ancient Near East. The Exodus event is so momentous in Jewish history that it has often been called the "Gospel of the Old Testament." It was the foundational salvation event in Hebrew history that gave birth to the Jewish nation.

Scholars generally recognize the Song of the Sea as one of the oldest compositions found in the Hebrew Bible. The Song of the Sea is written in archaic Hebrew, consisting of a hymn (vss. 1-3), a short narrative (vss. 4-12) and a closing note on the victory (vss. 13-18). Its archaic appearance is important, since the first few books of the Bible are under fire by some scholars who claim that they were not written until very late in Israel's history.

The antiquity of the song is attested by several elements. Alan Cole identifies the word for "praise" in verse 2 as a *haepax legomenon* (a word that appears only once in the Bible), arguing that it "is one of the many archaisms of the song" (Cole, 1973, p. 131). Additional examples include archaic suffixes on the Hebrew verbs "destroy" (vs. 9) and "swallowed" (vs. 12), and the phrases "holy habitation" and "sanctuary" in vss. 13 and 17, respectively (pp. 131-132).

A consensus of scholars have dated the song no later than the 10th century B.C. W.F. Albright dated the composition to the 13th century B.C. (1957), while, more recently, Brian Russell has dated it to about 1150 B.C. (2007). Widely respected scholars Frank Moore Cross and David Noel Freedman date the song no later than the 10th century.

Writing in 1997, Freedman flatly states:

> I am as firmly convinced today as I was forty-five years ago that early [Hebrew] poems really are early. While it is true that many, perhaps most, serious scholars date this poetry across the whole spectrum of Israelite history, ... I believe that the whole corpus belongs to the earliest period of Israel's national existence, and that the poems were composed between the twelfth and tenth-ninth centuries B.C.E. I have encountered neither compelling evidence nor convincing argument to the contrary, or to make me think otherwise (Cross and Freedman, 1997, p.x.).

While scholars generally date the song very early, many still date it several centuries after the time of Moses. However, there is solid evidence that supports the belief that Moses could have written the song himself. This includes Egyptian language in the song, which would be only natural since Moses would have been trained in an Egyptian school called the k3p, or 'the Royal Nursery,' where foreign-born princes were educated. [NOTE: Despite the use of the word 'nursery,' this school was a prestigious one — some prominent Egyptian government officials listed their attendance in the Royal Nursery in their 'resumes' recorded on the walls of their tombs. Cf. Acts 7:22] This connection is strengthened by the fact that the language in Exodus 15:4 includes the formal Egyptian phrase 'of the choicest' and the word often translated 'captions,' both of which have Egyptian parallels (Craigie, 1970, pp. 84-85). In order to use this language, whoever wrote it must have been trained in Egypt. This provides a perfect fit for the biblical account of Israel's presence in Egypt.[4]

The words of the Song of the Sea are indeed instructive. Verses 1-7 are consistent with the suggestion made in Chapter Six that the Egyptian host was thrown into the sea from a high place, i.e., a dam/roadway. Only verses 8 and 10 are consistent with the cinematography provided by Cecil B. DeMille's "The Ten Commandments." Verse 19, which is not technically part of the song, is ambivalent; it could apply to either "picture." However the song of Miriam, in verse 21, which is repetitive of the initial verses, reinforces the suggestion and analysis of verses 1-7 that the Egyptian host was thrown into the sea from a high spot.

Regardless of whether Miriam wrote the Song of the Sea in full or in large part and whether she contributed in the composition of the Hymn to the Aten, it is apparent that Moses/Akhenaten and Miriam/Nefertiti worked together as a team.

It is rather poetic that Miriam's participation in the Exodus story is almost always tied to water: 1) She is present with Moses/Akhenaten in the bulrushes in the water at his infancy; 2) she is the poet and songstress after the ambush and destruction of Pharaoh Ramses I at Yam Suph; and 3) at her death, she is tied to "Miriam's well," which provides water to the people of the Exodus.

Before leaving the subject of the Song of the Sea, it is important to note the following. Exodus 15:20 indicates that Miriam is a "prophetess." She is said to be the sister of Aaron, with no reference being made to Moses/Akhenaten. This is a distinct effort to separate Miriam/Nefertiti from Moses/Akhenaten because, if it were not deliberate, she should have been described as being "the sister of *Moses and* Aaron." The Torah elevates her to the status of prophetess well before it conveys that same status upon Moses/Akhenaten. In fact, Moses is only called a prophet on two occasions. Moses/Akhenaten is referred to as a prophet somewhat obliquely in Numbers 12:6-8, and, later, directly in one of the very last verses of Deuteronomy. Deuteronomy 34:10 states: "there hath not risen a prophet since in Israel like unto Moses." If nothing else, Miriam/Nefertiti was joined at the hip to Moses/Akhenaten by the identical references to them as being prophets.

In sum, unlike her mother-in-law, Queen Tiye, who was only interested in maintaining power and family control of the Egyptian throne, Miriam/Nefertiti was a pillar of strength for Moses/Akhenaten. She was a leader of her people and, most importantly, she was a partner with her husband in creating a future for her people.

9

DEATH OF MOSES

While the Torah indicates the age of Moses at his death to have been 120 years, I believe that number is allegorical only. The significance of this number in Judaism is that people who live to be 120 years are considered to have lived a full, or more than a full, life. Even today, a Jewish expression is: "May you live to be 120 years." Osman suggests that Moses actually died when he was approximately 62 to 65 years old at the hands of Pharaoh Seti I, the son of Ramses I. Between the incidents of the ambush, the death of his father at Yam Suph and the raiding of one or more Egyptian fortresses for water, Seti I was driven to seek revenge. Osman sets forth his view of the death of Moses:

> A reference to a confrontation between him and the "Angel of Death" on the Mount before he died, with an indication of a struggle between the two, has persuaded some biblical scholars that Moses was killed ... by his own followers for being too rigid in his views. I do not think this is an accurate interpretation of what happened.

> The key, it seems to me, lies in the reason given why Moses was not allowed to enter Canaan, the Promised Land. According to the Book of Exodus, the reason is that Moses struck a rock with his rod to obtain water for his thirsty followers. This is not really convincing. Why should this practical action be the cause of punishment? It is not as if there is any suggestion that he had

been forbidden to indulge in such conduct.

However, when we look back at the wars of Seti I, the second king of the Nineteenth Dynasty, against the Shasu we find that the first confrontation took place in the vicinity of one of the Egyptian fortresses on the route between Zarw and Gaza. Such fortresses were built in areas that had wells. It would therefore seem to be a more likely explanation — even if it can be only supposition — that Moses, under pressure from his thirsty followers, entered one or more of these fortresses and obtained water by using his royal scepter. Intrusions of this type would have been reported by the Egyptian guards to their superiors at Zarw, resulting in Seti I sallying forth to put a stop to the unrest that the Shasu were causing among the Sinai settlements. After the initial battle, Seti I, as we saw earlier, chased the Shasu, identified as the Israelites, into northern Sinai —and, if these Talmudic references to the death of Moses are correct, it must have been there that Moses died, out of sight of his followers, most probably at the hand of Seti I.[1]

Osman's supposition has some support in the Torah. As we previously noted, Numbers 20:1 reports the death of Miriam. But the very next verse juxtaposes the report of her death with a search for water. Verse 2 states: "And there was no water for the congregation." If the death of Miriam/Nefertiti related to a search for drinking water, it would have paralleled the suggested death of Moses/Akhenaten by Osman.

The life of Miriam/Nefertiti was related to water in three ways, as noted in the preceding chapter: 1) The Torah story of the birth of Moses relates that his sister hid him in the waters; 2) the death of the pursuing Egyptians at Yam Suph is celebrated by the Song of the Sea, composed at least in part by Miriam/Nefertiti; and 3) the above story which expands, in Jewish lore, to the parable of a well of water (Miriam's well) which does not abandon the Hebrews in all their years of wandering, but accompanies them on all their marches.

The death of Aaron is reported in the Torah shortly after the death of Miriam. According to Numbers 20:22-29, his place of death was at a mountaintop. Verse 24 states that: "Aaron shall not enter into the land which I have given unto the children of Israel, because you [Aaron] rebelled against My word at the *waters* of Meribah."

The place of death of Moses is suggested in the Torah, in Deuteronomy 32:49-52, which also makes reference to the waters of Meribah.

All of the foregoing references to water support Osman's supposition that Moses, under pressure from his thirsty followers, entered one or more of the outlying Egyptian fortresses and obtained water. Seti I may have indeed chased Moses/Akhenaten and his followers into Northern Sinai and killed Moses/Akhenaten on a mountaintop.

But there is a postscript to this story. Friedman makes reference to a veil of Moses. (See also Exodus 34:33-35.) In describing the story of the revelation at

Mount Sinai, Friedman reports "that there is something unusual about Moses' face when he comes down from the mountain. When the people see him they are afraid to come near him. Moses therefore wears a veil from then on whenever he speaks to the people." Friedman then asks: "What is it about Moses' face in the Priestly source?"[2]

He gives an explanation; but I think there is a better explanation for wearing the veil. When Moses/Akhenaten died, Miriam/Nefertiti and Aaron were already dead. Moses/Akhenaten was the last of the initial leaders of the peoples of the Exodus. It would have been difficult to lead a contentious group of people, as the Torah describes the Hebrews, without firm authority. I suggest that, after Moses died, a "stand-in" may have filled his place and worn a veil for a disguise. The perception of the people of the Exodus that they were still in the presence of their leader Moses/Akhenaten would have given strength to them, and their new leaders, during their continuing travails in the desert.

The foregoing reference to, and explanation for, a veil may further relate to the discussion of the khepresh in Chapter Seven, Section VII. As earlier suggested, the khepresh evolved during the lifetime of Moses/Akhenaten from being a sign of monarchy to a sign of authority for Moses and for Levites, such as Aaron/Meryare II and Pinchas. It is possible (and perhaps even likely) that the tail-end of the cloth used to create the headdress may have been used to wrap around the face of the person in authority wearing it. This would have also have limited the possibility that persons, who were passersby of the encampments, would have been able to positively report to the sitting pharaoh that Moses/Akhenaten had been found. They would only have been able to report that a group of men in the camp, who appeared to be in authority, were seen wearing a khepresh-style head covering. The change in usage of the khepresh could have been explained to Hebrews in the encampment as a result of health concerns for avoiding blowing sand or sunburn. The "veil," therefore, would not have been a separate instrument of clothing, but merely a part of the headdress used as facial covering. Between the headdress, the "veil" and a beard, a "stand-in" for Moses/Akhenaten could have easily lived within the encampments. Finally, use of the "veil" would have resulted in disguising the tonal or vocal quality of any utterances made by the stand-in.

The illusion that Moses/Akhenaten was still alive and leading his people may have been crucial to the survival of the Hebrews and the viability of their future. Moses and the Hebrews are said to have wandered the desert for forty years. One common reason given for this is that the period of wandering was the time necessary to erase any remnant of slave mentality in the Hebrew population. While this may be true, it is perhaps more likely that it was the period necessary for forging a new nation from a disparate group of people. So long as the people believed that Moses was still alive and in their physical presence, they could carry on the process of creating a new nation. Through the stand-in who wore the veil, the spirit of Moses was, in fact, still alive and with the people.

The Torah indicates that the burial place of Moses was not known to the people of the Exodus. The commentaries to the Torah indicate that this was important because it ensured that the burial place would not become a place of pilgrimage and result in the elevation of Moses to a deity. This does not ring true because the burial places of others — such as the Cave of the Patriarchs (Cave of Machpelah) in Hebron, which is the alleged burial site of Abraham, Isaac, Jacob, Sarah, Rebecca and Leah[m] — have not resulted in deification of the patriarchs, matriarchs, or any such other deceased leader.

Whether the burial place of Moses/Akhenaten is not known because his remains were disposed by Pharaoh Seti I, disposed by the Hebrew survivors or, for any reason, left unfound in an unknown place, the result is the same. The Egyptians would not have wanted to elevate that site to a place of great honor because, in their opinion, he remained the Fallen One of Amarna. Similarly, the surviving Levites would not have wanted to call attention to future generations of any possible relationship between the Pharaoh Akhenaten and the Hebrew hero Moses.

At the end of Deuteronomy, the Torah refers to the greatness of Moses/Akhenaten: "There hath not risen a prophet since in Israel like unto Moses" (Deuteronomy 34:10). However, the Torah also deals throughout with the flaws and limitations of Moses/Akhenaten. The Torah shows his extreme anger when he destroys the first set of tablets containing the Ten Commandments. It shows his frustration at the site of Yam Suph when he asks God to show a favorable sign to the Hebrews. It shows us that he fought with his compatriots. It states that God, at one point, wanted to kill Moses. It seems that at times Moses/Akhenaten was a very difficult person with whom to deal.

Not only was he difficult, but he was also complex. I have earlier suggested that Moses/Akhenaten was very much in love with his sister-wife, Miriam/Nefertiti. There is evidence shown in existing murals that, at the time before his abdication, he was also a very loving father and actively engaged in the youthful activities and upbringing of his daughters. However, after the first exile (before the Exodus), there is little evidence in the Torah of his personal life. Thereafter, there is, substantially, only the personal incident of the "Cushite wife." It is possible that his changed status after the Exodus led to a withdrawal by Moses/Akhenaten from personal relationships with his family. But it is equally possible that he maintained those relationships and that those relationships were not recorded because they were not significant for purposes of recording the process of molding the ethnicity and religious identity of the Hebrew people.

There are many misconceptions about Moses/Akhenaten. A better understanding of the complexities of his life and personality allows us to clear up some of those misconceptions. There has been speculation that Akhenaten/Moses suffered from medical deficiencies and illnesses and that those illnesses explained

---

m   Rachael was buried elsewhere; the Torah indicates that she was buried near Bethlehem.

his apparently androgynous appearance. However, there are statues in existence which belie that conclusion; he was not physically misshapen. (In this regard, see the photo in Appendix I, figure 3.) It is probably more believable that, in contemplating a non-corporeal God and in projecting equality with the women in his life (primarily Nefertiti/Miriam), he reached a theological conclusion that God has no sexual identity and that God was equally God to both male and female humans. Since Akhenaten/Moses was the high priest of Atenism at that time, he would have initially projected an androgynous appearance of himself similar to that which he projected to his god, Aten.

Some might find it totally unconvincing that the Pharaoh Akhenaten would have abdicated from his throne. After all, he had been the supreme ruler of the finest empire and civilization of his time. He had also been the high priest, who was the sole direct connection to his god, the Aten. Is it reasonable to assume that he would abdicate and go into exile? The answer is yes. We can point to several historical examples that mirror this circumstance.

First, King Edward VIII of England abdicated the throne in order to marry the woman he loved, Wallis Simpson. He remained married to her until his death thirty-five years later. Second, the current Dalai Lama went into exile in order to protest the occupation of his country, Tibet, by China and as a means of perpetuating the religion of the Tibetan people. Third, Robert E. Lee, who became the Chief General of the Confederacy, resigned his commission as an officer in the United States Army and rejected an offer to be the Supreme Commander of the Northern Army of the United States. He fought long and valiantly to protect his native State of Virginia as part of the Confederacy. After his surrender to General Ulysses S. Grant, he spent the balance of his life trying to heal the wounds that had been created, partly by his own actions, during the Civil War.

Others might find it totally unconvincing that a man of God, such as Moses, could have also been a despotic pharaoh of Egypt. Is it reasonable to assume that Moses and Pharaoh Akhenaten were one and the same person? Again, the answer is "yes." We have multiple instances which "fit" the circumstance. First, Richard M. Nixon, who we might also note resigned from a position of great authority, was a virulent anti-communist; however, he was conversely the creator of a détente with the communist Republic of China. Second, and closer to home for the Jewish people, Menachem Begin, who in his youth was the leader of a Zionist militant group, won the Nobel Prize for Peace because he, along with Anwar Sadat, forged a peace treaty between Israel and Egypt.

In each of the foregoing cases, we find that people in power will, under unique circumstances, resign or, in the case of Akhenaten/Moses, abdicate. As earlier suggested, if Akhenaten/Moses had not abdicated, he would have been killed and his religious creation of Atenism and, subsequently, of his new religion of Judaism, would have died. Further, as earlier suggested, if Akhenaten/Moses had not changed his psyche from that of a monarchical ruler to that of a partner with

Aaron and Levites in creating a new theology, his religion of Judaism might also, upon his death, have died with him. Under these circumstances, it is quite possible he would have abdicated the throne and changed his persona to ensure the viability of his unique religious belief and his perceived connection to his monotheistic God, Adonai [YHWH].

Despite his complexities, Moses/Akhenaten was a giant in stature as a religious theorist. This is evidenced, perhaps, by the transmogrification of the pharaonic concept of the king being divine, to the Judaic concept of God being King. For example, in one of the three prayers of confession recited during the Jewish High Holy Days, Avinu Malkeinu, we pray to "our Father, our King." In any event, it would be hard to believe that any other person could have taken the tortuous path from being a pharaoh of Egypt to being the father of Judaism and forefather of Christianity and Islam. Nor is it likely that any other person could have traveled the tortuous path from a belief in a fatalistic, cyclical religious theory of birth and death, as promulgated by Egyptian pantheistic religions, to a new theology — one which posits that a singular and unique God is experienced in the flow of history, that human participation in that flow is a necessary ingredient and that such human participation must be an expression of ethical conduct. This personal and theological history establishes the greatness of Moses/Akhenaten and explains why "there hath not risen a prophet since in Israel like unto Moses." It explains why the Torah comprises a compendium of five books (scrolls) in which the dominant unifying personage was Moses/Akhenaten.

The theology and religion of Moses/Akhenaten and his Levite compatriots, as given effect through the prayers, rituals, customs and practices referred to in this book, is the true Legacy of Moses and Akhenaten.

EPILOGUE

My motivation in writing this work comes from my personal history. My father, David, died when I was 13, just after my Bar Mitzvah. But, unlike many Jewish children, I continued my Jewish education. For a short time, I attended the Chicago Jewish Academy, then the only local Jewish religious-secular high school in the area.

Annually, our family, consisting of my mother, Celia, my sister and brother-in-law, Barbara and Herbert, and myself, participated in large Passover Seders. My mother's oldest brother, Nathan Kessler, was the *pater familias* of my maternal family and, as such, conducted a Seder on the first night of Passover for approximately thirty members of the extended family. When his health began to fail, he appointed me to continue the family Passover tradition.

My mother married Harold Pattis. We attended Seders for that family on the second night of Passover at the home of the father-in-law of my (step)brother, David Pattis. David's father-in-law, Lewis Shaffer, was the pater familias of that extended family. When his health, too, began to fail, he appointed me to continue the Passover tradition of that extended family. When he died, my brother and sister-in-law, Muriel, agreed to continue to host the second Seder, provided that I would continue to lead the ceremonies.

As a result, I have led one or two Seders each year for nearly sixty years. At times, I felt like the composer Nikolai Rimsky-Korsakov, who, after being appointed Professor of Music, prepared his lessons for his students by learning the materials the night before the classes which he taught. Annually, I dealt with reviewing and analyzing the text of the Haggadah, the liturgical book for the Seder. The word "Seder" means "Order," but when I examined the Haggadah, it seemed anything but ordered. So, one of my first efforts was to attempt to give more meaning and significance to the Seder ceremony. I then began to consider the historical and theological underpinnings of the Haggadah.

Abba Eban, in his book *My People, the Story of the Jews*, was an early source for reflection. He wrote:

> The Mosaic concept of divinity [as distinguished from that of Abraham] is less intimate and naive, more austere, but far more sublime. Moses is capable of an unprecedented exercise in abstraction. He can envision a God above nature, immune from human passion and natural vicissitudes. The pagan concept of history as tied inexorably to the wheel of repetition imparts a profound melancholy to most of ancient thought. [This is reflected in] the despairing cry of the Roman philosopher, Marcus Aurelius: "Up and down, to and fro, round and round, this is the monotonous and meaningless rhythm of the universe." Against the characteristic fatalism of pagan civilizations, Hebrew thought, from Moses onward, conceives of God as the author of natural forces, exempt from their cyclical rhythm. The divine purpose fulfills itself not in nature, but in human history. ...
>
> Once human destiny is separated from the cycle of nature, it breaks loose from the fatalistic chain of recurrence. Man has the capacity to "reject evil and choose good." He is thus endowed with a unique and active dignity, beyond the reach of any other element in nature.[1]

Jill and Leon Uris, in the book *Jerusalem*, provided a slightly different insight. They wrote that the "laws of science, Moses deduced, were absolute." They continued:

> Life around [Moses] consisted of many absolutes. ... The close inspection of insects, flowers, animal life showed them made up functional absolutes. All of these were part of the universal system of order.
>
> Moses' ... search left him to conclude that there were moral laws as well as laws of science and nature. These laws, however, were unseen by the naked eye nor could they be proved by the addition or subtraction of numbers. It was man's duty to discover what these moral laws were. ... There were, indeed, certain universal rights and wrongs.
>
> Moses became the first man we know of to apply the theory of force and counterforce. He knew that every force of evil would be met by a counterforce of good and that these forces would be in eternal conflict. They could and did coexist within a single man, a tribe or an entire nation. Only if a universal moral law could be defined and accepted ... could man actually know right from wrong.[2]

I would express the reflections of Jill and Leon Uris somewhat differently and suggest that, rather than moral *laws*, a better expression would be: moral *rules*. In any event, the concept of rules (or laws) of morality directly ties into *ethical monotheism*.

I began to understand the significance of the portion of the Haggadah which states that: "In every generation one must look upon himself as if he had personally come out from Egypt, as the Bible says: 'Thou shall tell thy son on that day, saying: It is because of that which the Eternal did for *me* when I went forth from Egypt,' for it was not alone our forefathers whom the holy one … redeemed; he redeemed *us* too" (emphasis in original).[3] As part of ethical monotheism, we, as Jews, are responsible for our actions and our relationships with other human beings.

After a number of years, I compiled my own Haggadah and, in so doing, took the position that the text was not static in nature, but could be modified, shortened, or lengthened to reflect new insights and, also, changes in Jewish and in world history. I added a reference to the Holocaust, which I tied to the portion of the text dealing with the prophet Elijah. I added a fourth matzah to the normal ceremonial plate of three matzahs, as a connection to segments of world Jewry which continue to experience oppression and cannot otherwise express their relationship with their religious brethren. I adopted the practice of adding a cup of water to memorialize the contributions of Miriam to the story of the Exodus and to the beginnings and survival of Judaism.

Additional sources caused an even more intensive review. First, Philip Glass, the composer, wrote a magnificent opera entitled "Akhnaten." In the liner notes was a historical perspective by Shalom Goldman dealing with the Amarna period. I attempted to create a timeline with respect to the lives of, and inter-relationships between, Akhenaten and Moses. My research initially led to a conclusion that Akhenaten lived approximately one hundred years before Moses. That initial conclusion was one I revisited over a period of time. I then reached a new conclusion that Moses and Akhenaten were the same person. That new conclusion is the basis for this book. Second, I acquired a book by Shmuel Safrai and his son, Ze'ef Safrai, entitled *Haggadah of the Sages*, which showed an evolution of the text of the Haggadah over the course of many centuries. This book further whetted my appetite to investigate the evolution of the contents of the Haggadah and, thereby, the evolution of the story of the Exodus. Third, Simcha Jacobovici, who as noted has hosted a television series called "The Naked Archeologist," presented a television documentary, "The Exodus Decoded," which seemed to show that the descent of the Hebrews into Egypt correlated with the Hyksos domination of Egypt approximately 200 to 350 years before the timeline which I had then previously considered. This contradicted my earlier beliefs and, so, further stimulated my inquiries.

I had also become acquainted with and stimulated by the work of Richard Elliott Friedman.

I pursued my research online and found that Ahmed Osman and Charles Pope had written extensively on the subject of Moses/Akhenaten. I further pursued translations of the Torah and references to the Talmud. From all that, I was drawn to the analysis of Ahmed Osman, Moustafa Gadalla, and Charles Pope regarding the very convincing identification that Yuya was the same person as Joseph, the son of Jacob. Analysis of these and other materials led to the above noted conclusion that Moses and Akhenaten were the same person and that he was the grandson of Yuya (Joseph).

I began to integrate all of the foregoing materials.

Independently and on another "timeline," my wife Ronda (and one of my daughters, Lauren) were told by others that they bore a marked facial resemblance to Nefertiti. So approximately thirty to thirty-five years ago, I purchased a bust of Queen Nefertiti which, because of the (alleged) resemblance, has been placed prominently on display in our home since that time. When I reached the conclusion that Moses and Akhenaten were one and the same and that his spouse was Nefertiti, I jokingly considered the possibility that my wife was descended from a Queen. In any event, this aspect of our family life caused my continuing research to become highly personal.

Also, I have undertaken to teach some of my grandchildren their Bar and Bat Mitzvah lessons. Like Rimsky Korsakov, I was challenged to intensify my research so as not to be embarrassed by their questions. Certainly, it was and is my goal to cause them to internalize the studies of their heritage so that they conduct their Bar and Bat Mitzvah ceremonies as a vibrant part of their individual personas. I personally detest comments to a Bar or Bat Mitzvah child that: "You did a good *job.*" That expression connotes, in part, that the child's efforts were mostly "work." I would prefer a comment to such a celebrant that: "You are inspiring; you certainly have learned your heritage." That statement is more fitting.

Having concluded this effort, I first thank my wife, Ronda, for her patient (and sometimes reluctant) participation in the writing of this book. She has given me a sounding board, but, more importantly, an insight into the psychological motivations of the historical personages. Second, as noted, our children (David, Lauren and Michelle) and our grandchildren have provided a challenge and a goal. I was driven by the desire to give my grandchildren an opportunity to absorb Jewish history and heritage and make that history and heritage an integral part of their lives. I particularly thank my son-in-law, Nino, for his assistance in analyzing and diagramming my explanation of the drowning of the pharaoh and his hosts and, further, my explanation of the successful escape from Egypt.

I thank my dear friends and paralegals, Denise (who, at the date of this writing, has worked with me for 29 years), Laura (who, at the date of this writing, has worked with me for 15 years) and Sherry (who, at the date of this writing, has worked with me for 7 years). Basilios Stavros has proven to be a source of intellectual stimulation because of "playing out" the historical competition and interactions between Jews and Greeks. Michael R. Donahue insisted on editing and reviewing the text of this book and his commitment is appreciated. In the office, the book and the pace of its completion became a source of real interest and involvement. I thank all the members of the office staff.

I conclude with a reference to Rabbi Hillel, the rabbinic scholar. He summarized his understanding of Judaism with the following statement: "That which is hateful to you, do not do to your neighbor; That is the whole Torah. The rest is commentary." I would add, as a further touchstone of Judaism, the question: "Why?" It is a duty on the part of Jews to ask questions. Abraham questioned God regarding the destruction of the cities of Sodom and Gomorrah. Moses repeatedly questioned God. In current times, the composer Leonard Bernstein, in his third symphony, questions God. On a more mundane level, I too have questioned the text and meaning of the Torah.

In answer, I have concluded that, at least for me and my family, Judaism is a positive and integral part of our lives. However, I do not suggest that this book sets forth final answers. My hope is that others will be stimulated to ask additional questions and to provide more and better understandings of our Jewish heritage. I hope that these understandings will give greater insights and direction to us and to all who follow after us.

APPENDIX 1:

PICTURES

This appendix strongly relates to Chapter Three of this book.

Figure 1. Close-Up of Yuya

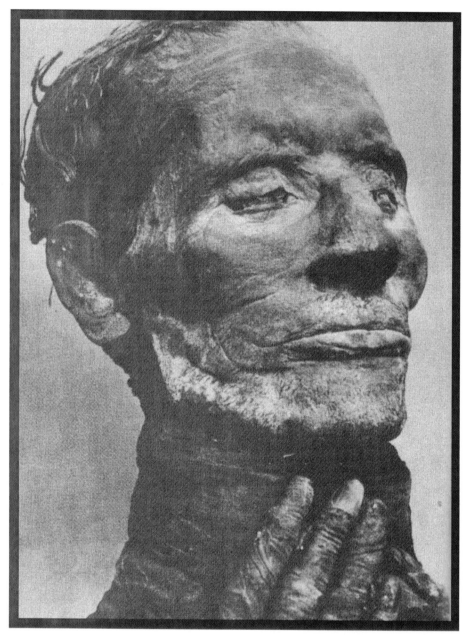

(Photo: Cairo Museum)

The above image shows a close-up of the mummy of Yuya. The position of the hands shows an acknowledgment of reverence, but is different from the required positioning of hands of royalty.

Figure 2. Yuya and Tuya

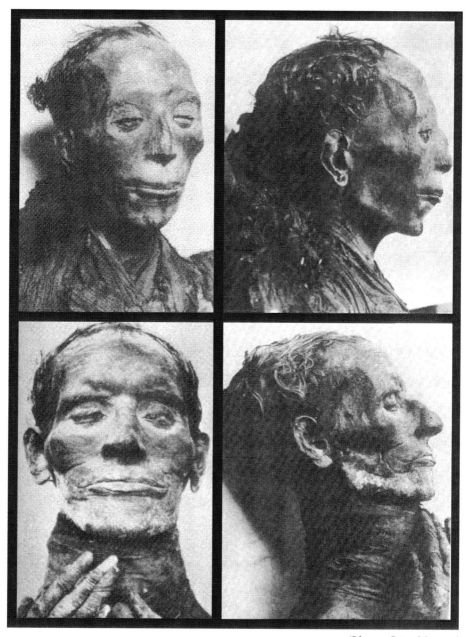

(Photos: Cairo Museum)

The above images show further pictures of Yuya and Tuya. Tuya's physiognomy is substantially different from that of her husband.

Figure 3. Akhenaten and Nefertiti

The above is a statuette of Akhenaten and Nefertiti housed at the Louvre that dates back to 1345–1337 BCE. Examination of the carving of Akhenaten indicates facial features which are less stylized than the famous representations that show very angular and elongated features. Further, his body shows no androgynous features. He has normal proportions. Queen Nefertiti was pretty, but not nearly the "beauty" that is represented in the famous bust of Nefertiti in Figure 4. Finally, note that he is wearing a khepresh (see discussion on p. 62).

To see this picture in color visit: http://**bit.ly/LOMAfig3** or scan the QR code with your mobile device.

Figure 4. Bust of Nefertiti

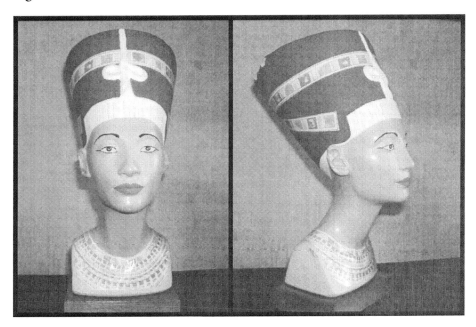

The images above show a frontal and side view of the famous bust of Nefertiti, showing very stylized beauty.

To see this picture in color visit: http://**bit.ly/LOMAfig4**
or scan the QR code with your mobile device.

Figure 5. Bust of Akhenaten

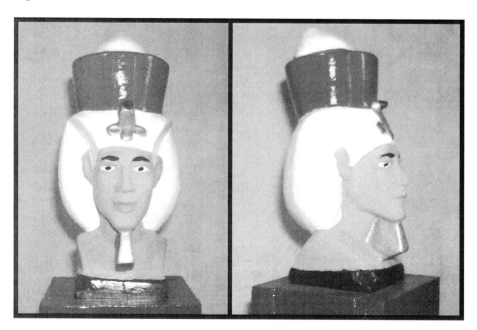

The images above show a representation of the Pharaoh Akhenaten. They show his prominent chin and are more stylized than the images in Figure 3. But they are not nearly as angular and harsh as other famous representations of the pharaoh.

To see this picture in color visit: http://**bit.ly/LOMAfig5** or scan the QR code with your mobile device.

Figure 6. Queen Tiye

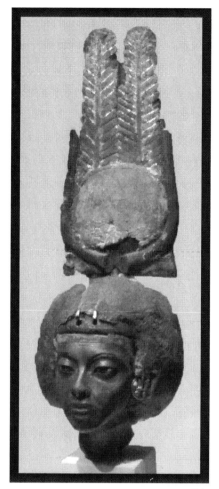

(Photo: Keith Schengili-Roberts)

The picture of Queen Tiye shows features consistent with Ethiopian heritage. Queen Tiye was the daughter of Yuya and Tuya.

To see this picture in color visit: http://**bit.ly/LOMAfig6** or scan the QR code with your mobile device.

Figure 7. Death Mask of Tutankhamun

(Photo: Matson Photo Service/Library of Congress)

A frontal view of the golden death mask of the Pharaoh Tutankhamun; Tutankhamun was the son of Akhenaten and the stepson of Nefertiti.

To see this picture in color visit: **http://bit.ly/LOMAfig7** or scan the QR code with your mobile device.

APPENDIX 11:

NUMBERING

This appendix relates to the subject matter of Chapter Five and is a commentary about the accuracy of the numbers reflected in the Torah.

In the following comments, Osman discusses discrepancies in the computation of years and other numerical counts. He notes that:

> One eminent biblical scholar who has commented on the length of the sojourn is the late Umberto Cassuto, formerly Professor of Biblical Studies at the Hebrew University of Jerusalem, who wrote: '... the numbers given in the Torah are mostly round or symbolic figures, and their purpose is to teach us something by their harmonious character ... these numbers are based on the sexagesimal system, which occupied in the ancient East a place similar to that of the decimal system in our days.

> 'The chronological unit in this system was a period of sixty years, which the Babylonians called a *sus*. One *sus* consisted of sixty years and two *sus* of a hundred and twenty years — a phrase that is used by Jews to this day. In order to convey that a given thing continued for a very long time, or comprised a large number of units, a round figure signifying a big amount according to the sexagesimal system was employed, for example, 600, 6,000, 600,000 or 300, 3,000, or 300,000 or 120, 360, 1,200, 3,600 and so forth. I further demonstrated there that, if it was desired to indicate a still larger amount, these figures were supplemented by seven or a multiple of seven.

The number 127, for instance (Genesis, 23:1), was based on this system.' Elsewhere Professor Cassuto makes the point that the figure forty, found frequently in the Bible, is similarly used as a kind of shorthand for a period of time and is not to be taken literally.[1]

As noted in the text of this book, direct reading of "numbers" often does not result in a satisfactory comprehension of history. In this regard, Osman and Professor Cassuto could have further expanded upon use of the number "40." It is perhaps significant that Moses is said to have ascended to Mount Sinai for forty days (Exodus 24:16-18) to receive the first set of tablets containing the Ten Commandments and, upon destruction of those tablets, to have ascended for a second period of forty days (Exodus 34:28). The wanderings in the desert are said to have taken forty years (Numbers 14:33-34). Perhaps it is easier to understand the text, from a historical perspective, as indicating that the two ascents to the top of Mount Sinai and the wanderings of the Hebrews before entering the land of Canaan were "shorthand for descriptions of extended periods of time and not numbers to be taken literally."

We can now correlate the relevant pharaohs of the Eighteenth Dynasty and their years of reign with corresponding Hebrew generations and their approximate dates of birth. The Egyptian list is more detailed and precise because the Egyptian histories and monuments are more fully documented.

Table 1 is largely self-explanatory. However, please note that the *length of reign* of the kings is reflected in the second column while the chronological identification for the Hebrew generations is based upon the *date of birth*. Also, please note that Levi, who was one of the sons of Jacob, was a brother to Yuya/Joseph. Yuya/Joseph was younger than Levi by approximately twelve years, so the date of his birth was about 1435. Yuya was appointed vizier (prime minister) by Tuthmosis IV in about 1412 and continued to serve under Amenhotep III until about 1375. In other words, he was closely allied to two consecutive pharaohs. Semenkhkare, who was apparently a half-brother of Akhenaten, was appointed by Akhenaten as a co-regent toward the end of his own reign. However, Semenkhkare only survived the end of the reign of Akhenaten by a short period, perhaps only a matter of days or weeks.

Table 1: Pharoahs of 18th and 19th Dynasties

King (18th Dynasty)	Length of Reign	Dates BCE	Hebrew Generation	Dates of Birth BCE
Tuthmosis III	54	1490–1436	Isaac Jacob Levi (Joseph)	1485 1466 1447 (1435)
Amenhotep II	23	1436–1413	Kohath	1428
Tuthmosis IV	8	1413–1405	Amram	1409
Amenhotep III	38	1405–1367	Aaron (Moses)	1390 (1385)
Akhenaten (alone)	6	1367–1361		
Semenkhkare	–	–		
Tutankhamun	9	1361–1352		
Aye	4	1352–1348		
Horemheb	13	1348–1335		
King (19th Dynasty)				
Ramses I	2	1335–1333		
Seti I	29	1333–1304		
Ramses II	67	1304–1237		

Table 2: Part of the Eighteenth Dynasty

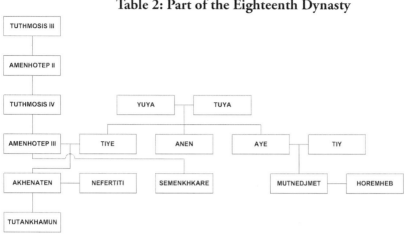

The Torah refers to four generations as existing between the date of the descent into Egypt and the date of the Exodus. They are identified as Levi, Kohath, Amram and Moses. While the last generation is identified as being that of Moses, it is more properly, in terms of genealogy, the generation of Aaron, because Aaron was a direct descendant of Levi. Conversely, Amram would have been the direct ancestor of Aaron and not of Moses. However, Akhenaten (or the writers of the Torah), in order to tie Akhenaten/Moses more directly to the genealogy of the descendants of Levi, connects Akhenaten to the Hebrew sequence of generations. While Amenhotep III was his *biological* father, Akhenaten gave the name Amran[n] to his *spiritual* "father," the Aten, as is set forth in a cartouche referring to Akhenaten's god.[o] Also note that the name "Amarna," which is the generalized term for the reign of Akhenaten, derives from the name Amran and the aforesaid adopted religious relationship.

The Torah also refers to the period of time between the descent into Egypt and the date of the Exodus in three ways: 1) four generations; 2) 400 years; or 3) 430 years. Osman more fully analyzes this "counting system" as contained within the Torah.[2] Suffice it to say at this point, that four generations is more properly related to an aggregate term of fifty to eighty years, rather than 400 or 430 years. Another way of looking at this is to ascribe 100 years, putatively, to each generation; this would account for the periods, otherwise described as being a total of 400 to 430 years, as being more correctly four generations.

---

n   Note that in Egyptian the name is Amran, while in Hebrew the name is Amram.

o   This correlates with the reference in the Torah to Amram being the father of Moses (Exodus 6:20 and Hertz, *Pentateuch and Haftorahs*, 214).

APPENDIX III:

SONG OF THE SEA

This appendix relates to Chapters Six and Eight of this book. They reflect the Song of the Sea, appearing in Exodus 15:1-21. These verses are as follows:

v 1   Then sang Moses and the children of Israel this song unto the Lord, and spoke, saying:
> I will sing unto the Lord, for He is highly exalted;
> The horse and his rider hath He thrown into the sea.

v 2   The Lord is my strength and song,
> And He is become my salvation;
> This is my God, and I will glorify Him;
> My father's God, and I will exalt Him.

v 3   The Lord is a man of war,
> The Lord is His name.

v 4   Pharaoh's chariots and his host hath He cast into the sea,
> And his chosen captains are sunk in the Red Sea.

v 5   The deeps cover them —
> They went down into the depths like a stone.

v 6   Thy right hand, O Lord, glorious in power,
> Thy right hand, O Lord, dasheth in pieces the enemy.

v 7 And in the greatness of Thine excellency Thou overthrowest them that
rise up against Thee;

Thou sendest forth Thy wrath, it consumeth them as stubble.

v 8 And with the blast of Thy nostrils the waters were piled up—

The floods stood upright as a heap;

The deeps were congealed in the heart of the sea.

v 9 The enemy said:

'I will pursue, I will overtake, I will divide the spoil;

My lust shall be satisfied upon them;

I will draw my sword, my hand shall destroy them'

v 10 Thou didst blow with Thy wind, the sea covered them;

They sank as lead in the mighty waters.

v 11 Who is like unto Thee, O Lord, among the mighty?

Who is like unto Thee, glorious in holiness,

Fearful in praises, doing wonders?

v 12 Thou stretchedst out Thy right hand —

The earth swallowed them.

v 13 Thou in Thy love has led the people that Thou hast redeemed;

Thou hast guided them in Thy strength to Thy holy habitation.

v 14 The peoples have heard, they tremble;

Pangs have taken hold on the inhabitants of Philistia.

v 15 Then were the chiefs of Edom affrighted;

The mighty men of Moab, trembling taketh hold upon them;

All the inhabitants of Canaan are melted away.

v 16 Terror and dread falleth upon them;

By the greatness of Thine arm they are as still as a stone;

Till Thy people pass over, O Lord,

Till the people pass over that Thou hast gotten.

v 17 Thou bringest them in, and plantest them in the mountain of Thine
inheritance,

The place, O Lord, which Thou hast made for Thee to dwell in,

The sanctuary, O Lord, which Thy hands have established.

v 18 The Lord shall reign for ever and ever.

v 19 For the horses of Pharaoh went in with his chariots and with his horsemen into the sea, and the Lord brought back the waters of the sea upon
them; but the children of Israel walked on dry land in the midst of the
sea.

v 20 And Miriam the prophetess, the sister of Aaron, took a timbrel in her hand; and all the women went out after her with timbrels and with dances.

v 21 And Miriam sang unto them:

Sing ye to the Lord, for He is highly exalted:

The horse and his rider hath He thrown into the sea.

It is significant that the Song of the Sea begins with an almost identical phraseology to the last two lines of verse 21; the last two lines are attributed to Miriam. Again, as the text in Chapter Eight suggests, Miriam may have written the entire song or contributed to much of its text.

Also, while analysts, for other purposes, have intensively reviewed the text and the interrelationship of words and of "figures of speech" within the text, for our purposes there is a simpler analysis. There is a change in the figures of speech used in verses 1-7; these verses suggest crashing down from a height into the water. The imagery used in verses 8-10 is different. These verses suggest the Cecil B. DeMille vision.

I believe that verses 8-10 are a later addition, or the work of a separate writer, because, as noted, Miriam's song reinstates and reinforces the figures of speech initially set forth in verses 1-7 in the Song of the Sea; these words strongly reinforce the picture of crashing down from a height into the water.

APPENDIX IV:

MAPS AND ENGINEERING

This appendix contains maps and engineering drawings which effectively constitute a supplement to Chapter Six. They identify, generally, the site of the successful Exodus from Egypt and the defeat of the pursuing Egyptian host led by Pharaoh Ramses I. The engineering drawings are intended to illustrate, in conjunction with the text of Chapter Six, the workings of a cofferdam and sluices.

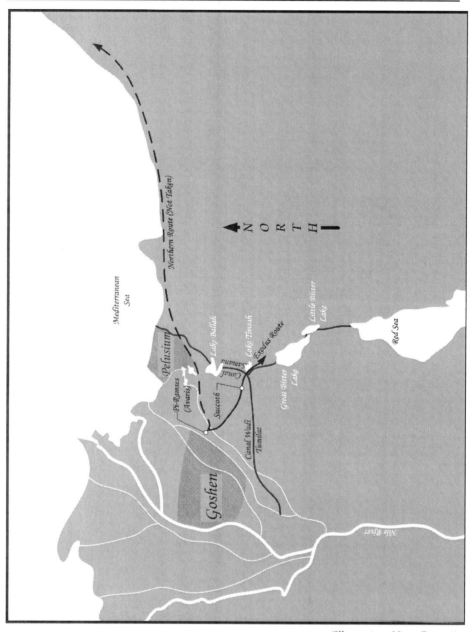

(Illustration: Nino Corsetti)

Illustration 1. Map of the Nile Delta, Canal Samana and Canal Wadi Tumilat

This illustration shows an area of northern Egypt generally circumscribed by the Mediterranean Sea on the north, the Canal Samana on the east, the Red Sea on the south and the Nile River and Nile River Delta on the west. Generally, navigational passage down the Nile could be made into the Mediterranean Sea. However, in order to utilize the Red Sea as a commercial body of water, it was necessary to connect an arm of the Nile River Delta to the Red Sea. This was accomplished by the construction of an east-west freshwater canal, called the Canal Wadi Tumilat. The eastern terminus of the Canal Wadi Tumilat tied into a southern freshwater canal, called the southern Canal Samana. The northern portion of the Canal Samana had commercial uses, but was apparently used equally as a water barrier. The water barrier prevented invasion from the east and, perhaps equally as important, it prevented escapes by disaffected residents from the interior of Egypt to refuge outside the country. North of the Canal Samana was the City of Pelusium, which was strategically located on one of the Nile branches at the Mediterranean Sea near the northern seacoast route. The northern seacoast route was also called the road of Horus.

When fully operational, the north-south Canal Samana utilized natural bodies of water, including Lake Ballah, Lake Timsah, Great Bitter Lake and Little Bitter Lake. Pi-Ramses (earlier known as Avaris) was a royal city which, according to the Torah, was the site of slave labor, imposed upon the Hebrews by the Egyptians, in order to build storehouses for the pharaoh.

The route taken by the Hebrews of the Exodus crossed the north-south Canal Samana, apparently just south of Lake Timsah and at the junction with the east-west Canal Wadi Tumilat. From there, the Hebrews traveled south and east into the heart of the Sinai Peninsula.

To see this picture in color visit: http://bit.ly/LOMAmap1 or scan the QR code with your mobile device.

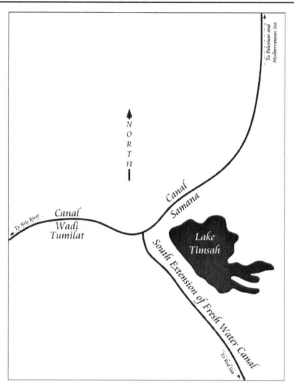

(Illustration: Nino Corsetti)

Illustration 2. Enlarged map of the junction between the east-west Canal Wadi Tumilat and the north-south Canal Samana

This junction of waterways fits the description in Exodus 13:3, where God says to Moses: "And Pharaoh will say of the children of Israel: They are entangled in the land, the wilderness hath shut them in." The suggestion from the Torah text would fit the reaction of pharaoh and his military host of pursuers. Once the Egyptians had information as to the route taken by Moses/Akhenaten and the Hebrews, they would have been inclined to believe that, being hemmed in by the junction of the two canals, there would be no escape route. Therefore, a speedy group of chariots and charioteers could have closed the gap with the Hebrews (who had had a head start). The Egyptians would have believed that the conditions would be favorable to capture and kill Akhenaten/Moses and many of his armed supporters, such as the coterie of military personnel or even the Levites. Without the leadership of Akhenaten/Moses and his supporters, the rest of the Hebrews would have been likely to surrender and return to servitude in Egypt. Certainly the complaining of the Hebrews suggests a mindset to return to Goshen.

To see this picture in color visit: http://bit.ly/LOMAmap2 or scan the QR code with your mobile device.

112

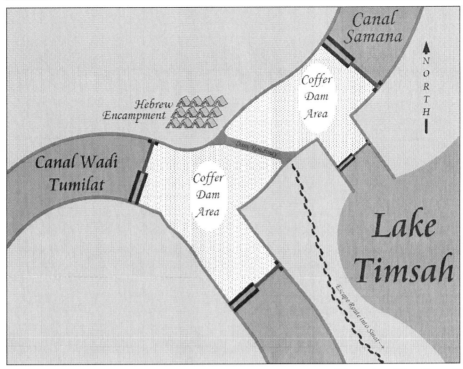

Illustration 3. Enlarged map of the area of the ambush by the Hebrews

The Hebrews camped in the evening on the northwest portion of the junction between Canal Wadi Tumilat and Canal Samana. They crossed the dam/roadway at night and later proceeded south and east into the Sinai. The cofferdam areas, when bled of their waters, would have assured that the Hebrews crossed on dry land and without easily falling off the roadway edge and into the water. In the morning, the Egyptians would have followed them across the dam/roadway and, having been stopped by barriers placed on the east side of the dam/roadway, they would have been trapped on the dam/roadway and imperiled by any oncoming rush of waters.

To see this picture in color visit: http://bit.ly/LOMAmap3 or scan the QR code with your mobile device.

113

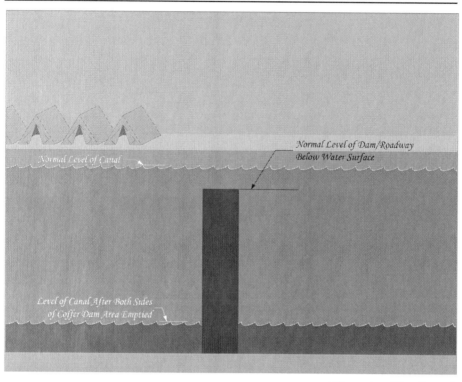

(Illustration: Nino Corsetti)

Illustration 4. Description of the normal level of the land surface, the normal edge of the canal depression and the water level being slightly over the dam/roadway

The normal level of the top of the dam/roadway would have been below the water's surface for purposes of providing clearance for riverboat traffic and, also, avoiding easy detection by any oncoming military host which would be inimical to the Egyptians. The level after both sides of the cofferdam area was emptied is shown at the bottom of the illustration.

To see this picture in color visit: http://bit.ly/LOMAmap4 or scan the QR code with your mobile device.

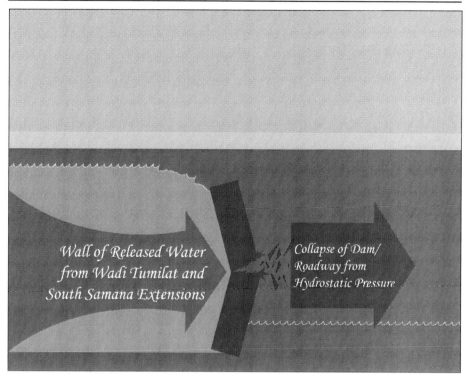

(Illustration: Nino Corsetti)

Illustration 5. Drawing showing the impact of released waters on one side of the dam/roadway and the collapse of that roadway from hydrostatic pressure

An onrush of waters on one side of the roadway would have created substantial hydrostatic pressures. As the roadway collapsed from the water pressure, any military personnel, chariots and charioteers then trapped on the surface of the dam/roadway would have been thrown, or "cast," into the water and drowned. Appendix III, which analyzes the text of the Song of the Sea, highlights the Torah terminology used to describe the drowning of the Egyptian host. The verbs used at the beginning of the Song of the Sea relate well to the depiction in this illustration.

To see this picture in color visit: http://bit.ly/LOMAmap5 or scan the QR code with your mobile device.

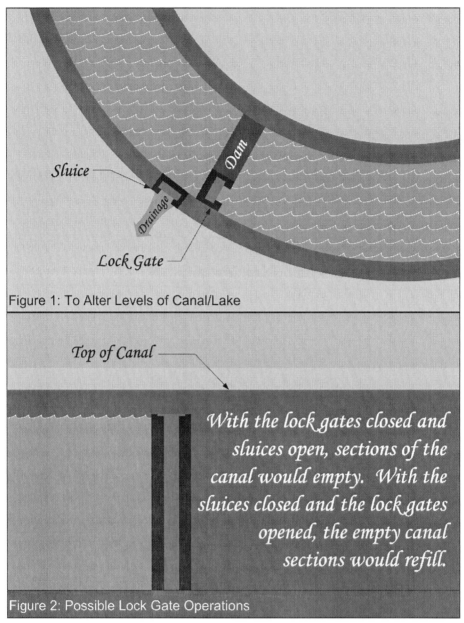

Figure 1: To Alter Levels of Canal/Lake

Sluice

Dam

Drainage

Lock Gate

Top of Canal

With the lock gates closed and sluices open, sections of the canal would empty. With the sluices closed and the lock gates opened, the empty canal sections would refill.

Figure 2: Possible Lock Gate Operations

(Illustration: Nino Corsetti)

Illustration 6. Drawing of mechanical sluices and dam locks, which may have been used in controlling water levels

One might question the source of the wood and stone for the sluices and locks, since part of the canals was in inhospitable desert-like regions. However, as noted in the text, Lake Timsah served as a commercial transshipment point. Accordingly, it would have been logical for the Egyptians to build warehouses in the Lake Timsah area. This would have permitted the Egyptians to store dam- and lock-construction materials, both for original installation and for repairs. The lake was perfectly located to serve as a warehouse and transshipment point for both the north and south portions of the Canal Samana and the eastern terminus of the Canal Wadi Tumilat.

There would have been sets of sluices and valve-like levers to drain or raise water from the canals and Lake Timsah. At least four sets of sluices and valves would have been required in this general area. They would have been located at the eastern terminus of the Canal Wadi Tumilat, the southern end of the northern portion of the Canal Samana, the northern end of the southern extension of the Canal Samana and the entranceway to Lake Timsah.

Because the level of Lake Timsah varied depending upon the time of the year and the (flood) level of the waters drained from the Nile River (the river which otherwise provided the primary source of water filling the canals), mechanisms of the cofferdams, sluices and valves would have been necessary to ensure that there was enough draft for commercial boats to use and traverse the canal/lake systems. Further, if a dry-dock system was utilized within the confines of Lake Timsah, as is suggested in the text by one of the quoted writers, it would have been necessary to use valves and sluices to raise and lower the water of the lake in order to use the dry-dock mechanisms. The drawing illustrates the mechanics of sluices and dams locks which may have been used by the Hebrews and Egyptians.

The historical sources indicate that, along the north-south Canal Samana, there were periodic watchtowers. These watchtowers could have been compromised by the Hebrews in one of two ways: 1) by the element of surprise, so that an attack at dusk or dawn would have been timed to overcome sleepy or relaxed watchmen; or 2) because the military personnel and engineers who were part of the Hebrew "mixed multitude" were Egyptian, they would have likely retained their "uniforms" and other military insignia. With such uniforms and insignia, the Hebrews would have easily blended in with the regular military personnel who otherwise would have been guarding the canals and the watchtowers and, consequently, the military arm of Moses/Akhenaten and his supporters would have been able to overcome the garrison positions in the watchtowers.

To see this picture in color visit: http://bit.ly/LOMAmap6 or scan the QR code with your mobile device.

APPENDIX V:

ISAAC'S PATERNITY

This appendix relates to Chapter Seven and deals with the relationship of Isaac to the Pharaoh Tuthmosis III.

Osman tells the story of the journey of Abram and Sarai to Egypt at a time of famine:

> Sarai was a beautiful woman and Abram was understandably afraid that he might be murdered if Pharaoh coveted her ... he took the precaution of suggesting: 'Tell them that you are my sister, so that I shall be treated well for your sake and my life will be spared because of you.' [Sarai] was taken to the Royal palace where she became Pharaoh's bride. ... The Lord 'inflicted serious diseases' on [Pharaoh] and his household, and, once he realized the cause of his problems, Pharaoh summoned Abram and asked ... Why didn't you tell me she is your wife? ... Here is your wife. Take her and be gone.'[1]

The story in the preceding paragraph is also confirmed in Genesis 12:12-19. Osman identifies the pharaoh as Tuthmosis III; he continues as follows:

> The Lord told Abram "... no longer will you be called Abram; your name will be Abraham, for I have made you a father of a host of nations ... kings will come from you." He also said: "Every male among you shall be circumcised." ... This command, which Abraham carried out, forged another link between the Hebrew tribe and Egypt, for, until that moment in history, only Egyptians among the eastern nations had adopted the custom of circumcision. At the same time, Sarai's name was changed as well. God said to Abraham: "As for Sarai your wife ... her name will be Sarah. I shall bless her and give you a son by her ... kings of peoples will come from her." *Sar*

in Hebrew means prince and *sarah* is the feminine form, which can even be interpreted to mean "the queen." ...

The promise that "kings of peoples" would descend from Sarah is the first mention of any Hebrew kings. ...

God [stated] ... "Your wife Sarah will bear you a son, and you will call him Isaac. I shall establish my covenant with him ..."

This passage makes it clear that Isaac was to be looked upon as Abraham's true heir. ... The critical question, upon which everything else turns, is: *Who was Isaac's father?* As Sarah was married to both Abraham and Pharaoh, the child could have belonged to either of them. However, if he was the son of Abraham, it is impossible to make any kind of logical and historical sense of the Old Testament story of Joseph and his family: it is only if Isaac was the son of Pharaoh, a prince of Egypt that everything else falls into place.

It is interesting in this context that the Talmud ... suggest[s] that, when born, Isaac did not look like Abraham: "On the day that Abraham weaned his son Isaac, he made a great banquet, and all the people of the world derided him, saying: 'Have you seen that old man and the woman who brought a foundling from the street, and now claim him as their son! And what is more they make a great banquet to establish their claim.'" The account then strikes a miraculous note, doubts about whether Isaac was actually Abraham's son having the result that "immediately the lineaments of Isaac's visage changed and became like Abraham's, whereupon they all cried out: 'Abraham begat Isaac.'"[2]

I am not certain if I agree that the above story about the birth of Isaac makes sense only if Isaac was the son of a pharaoh. It does, however, give an interesting insight into the historical beginnings of the Hebrews and the symbiotic relationship between the Hebrews and the ancient Egyptians.

There is a postscript to the preceding sentence. We have noted that sar means prince and that Sarah means princess or queen. This title appears to relate back to the status of Sarah as spouse of the pharaoh, because, inasmuch as the pharaoh was king, she became Queen. But, further, her grandson, Jacob, also had a name change – to Israel, Genesis 32:28 and Genesis 35:10. As Osman points out:

The Hebrew term *el* is the short form of Elohim (God) and *Ysra* or *sar* indicates a prince or a ruler. *Ysrael* means Elohim [God] rules. Pharaoh, too, was looked upon as a ruling god; therefore, Jacob's new name therefore connected him both with [Egyptian] Royalty and with his grandmother Sarah.[3]

There is yet another twist to this interrelationship. Osman suggests "that Tuthmosis IV was the pharaoh who appointed Yuya to the post of vizier. Tuthmosis IV seems to have been an Egyptian counterpart of Jacob and Joseph, a dreamer."[4] But if Osman is correct regarding genealogy, perhaps a better answer is that Tuthmosis IV recognized that Yuya was (or could have been) his cousin and, therefore, appointed him as vizier. After all, Yuya had (or might have had) royal blood.

So, we have seven generations of Hebrews directly tied to the Egyptian monarchy:

1. As to Abraham, his wife (Sarah) is also a spouse of Pharaoh Tuthmosis III;

2. Her son, Isaac, is quite possibly the son of the pharaoh, as noted above in the Talmudic story;

3. Isaac's son Jacob receives the "birth right" (or claim to pharonic royal descent) and has a name change to Israel, meaning Elohim [God] rules, which is a Hebrew translation of a title applicable to the pharaoh;

4. Jacob's son, Joseph, is possibly a cousin to Pharaoh Tuthmosis IV and is, more importantly, a *father to* pharaohs;

5. Joseph's daughter, Queen Tiye, becomes the Great Royal Wife of Amenhotep III and Joseph's son, Aye, becomes a (later) pharaoh;

6. Queen Tiye's son, Akhenaten, becomes a pharaoh;

7. Akhenaten's son, Tutankhamun, becomes a pharaoh.

The above establishes a truly symbiotic, if not direct, relationship between Hebrews and ancient Egyptian royalty.

APPENDIX VI:

AKEDAH
(THE BINDING OF ISAAC)

This appendix sets forth an analysis of the famous Torah portion which is called the Akedah. It relates to Chapter Seven.

The relevant portions of the Akedah (or The Binding of Isaac), from Genesis 22, are as follows:

v 2   Take now thy son, thine only son, whom thou lovest, even Isaac, and get thee into the land of Moriah; and offer him there for a burnt offering. …

v 3   And Abraham rose early in the morning, and saddled his ass, and took two of his young men with him, and Isaac his son; and he cleaved the wood for the burnt-offering, and rose up and went unto the place of which God had told him.

v 4   On the third day Abraham lifted up his eyes, and saw the place afar off.

v 5   And Abraham said unto his young men: "… I and the lad will go yonder; and we will worship, and come back to you."

v 6   And Abraham took the wood of the burnt-offering, and laid it upon Isaac his son; and he took in his hand the fire and the knife; and they went both of them together.

v 7   And Isaac spoke unto Abraham his father, and said: "My father." And he said: "Here am I, my son." And he said: "Behold the fire and the wood, but where is the lamb for a burnt-offering?"

v 8   And Abraham said: "God will provide Himself the lamb for a burnt-offering, my son." So they went both of them together.

v 9   … and Abraham built the altar there, and laid the wood in order, and bound Isaac his son, and laid him on the altar, upon the wood.

v 10   And Abraham stretched forth his hand, and took the knife to slay his son.

v 11   And the angel of the Lord called unto him … and said: "Abraham, Abraham …"

v 12   [The angel] said "Lay not thy hand upon the lad, neither do thou any thing unto him; for now I know that thou are a God-fearing man, seeing thou hast not withheld thy son, thine only son, from Me." …

v 15   And the angel of the Lord called unto Abraham a second time out of heaven,

v 16   And … saith the Lord, "because thou hast done this thing, and has not withheld thy son …

v 17   … I will multiply thy seed."

This portion is read every year on the second day of Rosh Hashanah. Hertz comments about this portion by stating: "The purpose of the command (to sacrifice Isaac) was to apply a supreme test to Abraham's faith."[1]

I disagree with his analysis and note that, in the earlier texts of Genesis 18:22-32, Abraham argues mightily with God about God's threat to destroy the cities of Sodom and Gomorrah. Abraham asks: "if there are fifty righteous people, would you not spare the city for the fifty righteous people?" God responds, "If I find in Sodom fifty righteous people, then I will save the city." Abraham presses on: "What if there are only forty-five righteous people?" And God responds, "I will not destroy the city if I find forty-five." Abraham presses and asks: "What about forty?" And God responds, "I will not do it if there are forty." Abraham continues and God responds in similar manner until God agrees that, if only ten righteous people are found there, he will not destroy the city. How is it that in Genesis 18 Abraham can argue vehemently, in a toe-to-toe manner, with God, and in Genesis 22, when the issue concerns sacrificing his son, he meekly submits without a single question?

If it was a test of Abraham, I think he failed it. But I do not think that God was testing Abraham.

Abraham's son, Isaac, acted appropriately. Isaac calls out and acknowledges Abraham's fatherhood; Isaac gives appropriate deference, as later required by the Ten Commandments, by acknowledging: "my *Father*." Isaac continues by questioning, "Where is the lamb for the burnt offering?" And Abraham *lies* to him. Abraham is then so intent about sacrificing his son that the angel of the Lord calls

Abraham not once, but twice, in order to stop Abraham from continuing with the murder. But God is not upset; God agrees to bless Abraham.

How is it that Isaac acts properly, but Abraham is congratulated for acting immorally and improperly and almost committing cold-blooded murder? This text has vexed people since time immemorial. Again, I submit that Abraham was not tested for his faith. Rather, he was tested for his ability to question and to act in a moral manner. Abraham failed the test because he did not ask or challenge God: "Why?"

In Judaism, we are required to ask "Why?" I think, therefore, that the Akedah should be interpreted as an allegorical test of the people of Israel. Do we challenge and do we act appropriately? Do we follow blindly the path of Abraham, who did not question, or do we rise to the occasion and search our souls to do the right thing? If we question and rise to the occasion to do that which is good, then it is very appropriate to read the Akedah on every Rosh Hashanah when we are to do personal soul-searching and introspection.

In Appendix V, we set forth Osman's comment about the birth of, and fatherhood pertaining to, Isaac. The Akedah also makes sense if Abraham was aware, or suspected, that Isaac was not his genetic son and that he was acting out his hostility toward, and rejection of, another man's offspring. But even this interpretation gives rise to questions. It is not sufficient that one is, genetically, the parent of a child. Parenthood relates to being *in loco parentis*. If we raise a child as our own, we are in fact the parent. So even under this analysis, Abraham fails the test of acting in a moral manner and of asking: "Why?"

One interesting thing about Judaism is that we do not idealize our heroes. We recognize Abraham's faults. We recognize the shortcomings of Isaac, Jacob, Joseph and Moses. To merely state that one or more of these heroes "passed" a test of faith to God by an inappropriate action is to validate the stupidity or inequity of the action taken by that person. So again, I believe that the real test of the Akedah is, allegorically, a test of the Jewish people who, each year, are called upon to be ever questioning of their own conduct.

APPENDIX VII:

PROHIBITED SEXUAL AND MARITAL RELATIONSHIPS

This appendix relates to Chapter Seven and sets forth prohibited sexual and marital relationships. The prohibited relationships are enumerated in Leviticus 18:6-21, as follows:

v 6   None of you shall approach to any that is near of kin to him, to uncover their nakedness; I am the Lord.

v 7   The nakedness of thy father, and the nakedness of thy mother, shalt thou not uncover: she is thy mother; thou shalt not uncover her nakedness.

v 8   The nakedness of thy father's wife shalt thou not uncover, it is thy father's nakedness.

v 9   The nakedness of thy sister, the daughter of thy father, or the daughter of thy mother, whether born at home, or born abroad, even their nakedness thou shalt not uncover.

v 10   The nakedness of thy son's daughter, or of thy daughter's daughter, even their nakedness thou shalt not uncover; for theirs is thine own nakedness.

v 11   The nakedness of thy father's wife's daughter, begotten of thy father, she is thy sister, thou shalt not uncover her nakedness.

v 12   Thou shalt not uncover the nakedness of thy father's sister, she is thy father's near kinswoman.

v 13 Thou shalt not uncover the nakedness of thy mother's sister; for she is thy mother's near kinswoman.

v 14 Thou shalt not uncover the nakedness of thy father's brother, thou shalt not approach to his wife; she is thine aunt.

v 15 Thou shalt not uncover the nakedness of thy daughter-in-law: she is thy son's wife; thou shalt not uncover her nakedness.

v 16 Thou shalt not uncover the nakedness of thy brother's wife; it is thy brother's nakedness.

v 17 Thou shalt not uncover the nakedness of a woman and her daughter; thou shalt not take her son's daughter, or her daughter's daughter, to uncover her nakedness; they are near kinswomen; it is lewdness.

v 18 And thou shalt not take a woman to her sister, to be a rival to her, to uncover her nakedness, beside the other in her lifetime.

v 19 And thou shalt not approach unto a woman to uncover her nakedness, as long as she is impure by her uncleanness.

v 20 And thou shalt not lie carnally with thy neighbor's wife, to defile thyself with her.

v 21 And thou shalt not give any of thy seed to set them apart to Molech, neither shalt thou profane the name of thy God; I am the Lord.

Verse 7 rejects the incestuous relationship of Akhenaten/Moses with his mother, Queen Tiye. Verse 18 rejects the incestuous relationship of Akhenaten/Moses and of Abraham with their sisters, being respectively Nefertiti/Miriam and Sarah.

Aaron/Meryare II and the Levite priesthood rejected the "genetic" experiments suggested in Chapters Four and Seven in the text quoted from Charles Pope. They may have determined that the "genetic" experiments were unacceptable in accordance with the following:

1. Psychologically, incest is emotionally repugnant and unacceptable; in this regard, the psychoanalytical treatises of Sigmund Freud are enlightening. The Levites concluded that it was morally repugnant and totally unacceptable to encourage a lifestyle through incest where, among other things, advantage could be taken of children and other defenseless people.

2. An insular arrangement for incestuous lifestyles would result in royalty or leadership being cut off from the masses because the gene pool would be circumscribed and limited. The Levites concluded that the relationship of humankind to God was to be removed from the incestuous genetic experiments to create a "super royalty." Aaron/Meryare II,

in his expression of disapproval about the "Cushite wife," rejected the approach of Queen Tiye, which was founded upon her desire to perpetuate her control of the Eighteenth Dynasty. When Moses/Akhenaten consorted with Queen Tiye, as reflected in the Talmud and Egyptian texts and even as hinted at in the Torah, those who later followed after Aaron/Meryare II and the original Levites concluded that the only way to stop a repetition and continuation of such relationships was to proscribe any such incestuous liaisons.

3.   Rather than improving the gene pool by genetic engineering, incest results in genetic defects and physical and medical disabilities.

There is a sequel to the prohibitions of sexual relationships and prohibited marriages. This is contained in Leviticus 18:22 which states, very tersely: "Thou shalt not lie with mankind, as with womankind; it is an abomination." These thoughts prohibiting male homosexuality are repeated in Leviticus 20:13: "And if a man lie with mankind, as with womankind, both of them have committed abomination; they shall surely be put to death."

The short sentences in Leviticus 18:22 and Leviticus 20:13 have caused great difficulties throughout history, so they deserve further analysis. An examination of the earlier quoted verses shows that they relate to *heterosexual* prohibitions. The insertion of a prohibition pertaining to male homosexuality appears, therefore, to be largely gratuitous. In this regard, if one posits that God has spoken and that the expressions contained in the verses are the immutable word of God, there is nothing to consider. However, if one considers that Leviticus was written by priests or scribes several hundred years after Moses/Akhenaten, it is more likely that the expressions against male homosexuality were a reflection of the mores of the Jewish society in the years of the fifth century (in approximately 450 BCE), rather than a reflection of values at the time of Moses/Akhenaten. The two sentences in Leviticus may well reflect Jewish "pushback" in the fifth century to Greek influences in the Jewish society of that time.

At various times, ancient Judaism was to some degree in competition with Hellenism (i.e. Greek philosophy and culture). The Greek philosophers stressed logic and the beauty of the physical body. These concepts competed with Jewish values pertaining to spirituality and to a requirement of doing good actions. These competitive interrelationships existed from at least the time of Moses/Akhenaten, as reflected in Chapter Four, in the connection made by Pope between the story of Moses/Akhenaten and the story of Oedipus. They continued as noted in Chapter Six in the text concerning Mycenae and in the text regarding the possible relocation of part of the Simeonite tribe to Sparta.

However, perhaps the most dramatic evidence of a connection exists between the format of the book of Deuteronomy and that of Hellenistic literary forms. One half of Deuteronomy consists of an exposition of laws. The other half sets forth the farewell speech of Moses. In the totality of the Torah, there is no parallel to the literary style of setting forth the lengthy farewell speech of Moses/Akhenaten. Friedman indicates that the book of Deuteronomy was "found" in the Temple of Solomon in 622 BCE, so that the latest date for usage of this literary device in the Torah was at least that date.[1]

There is a parallel use of this literary device in Greek literature. The most famous example is the funeral oration of Pericles in the history book of the Peloponnesian Wars by Thucydides. This book was written in the fifth century BCE, but appears to reflect earlier examples of this literary device. It is possible that the Greek tradition started with the works of Homer.

The interrelationships between Hellenism and Judaism further existed through the rule of Alexander the Great and, ultimately, through the Hasmonean rebellion against the Seleucid empire, and the victory against the Greeks by Judah Maccabee, in approximately 165 BCE.

Further interrelationships existed with respect to translation of the Tanakh from Hebrew into Greek, begun in the third century BCE by the Septuagint.

Returning to the analysis of the text concerning homosexuality, a quick review of sources, from the most respected scientific journals to the online encyclopedia Wikipedia, shows that homosexuality is not limited to humankind. It is found in various other living species, certainly among mammals and reptiles. It would appear that 10-17 percent of human beings are homosexual.

The Torah does *not* proscribe anal sex within the context of heterosexual marriage. So, it is not the "act" which is an "abomination." The Torah text merely indicates rejection and disapproval of the homosexual relationship. It was more important for Jews to perpetuate their existence as a people by following the Torah's admonition to be "fruitful and multiply" than to submit to, and follow, the Hellenistic lifestyle.

Under this analysis, currently discriminating against a significant percentage of the population in the *name of God* is inane. Certainly, if living things are all results of God's acts of creation, those who discriminate against homosexuals are *rejecting God by discriminating against God's handiwork and creations*. Such discrimination, if carried to a logical conclusion, would perhaps result in a circumstance where a widowed man, who no longer desires conjugal relationships with women, but who prefers to live with another man, might experience the removal of his children by legal or religious authorities because these authorities reject the widower's lifestyle. Such removal would give rise to a whole host of difficult questions. Therefore, it would appear to be more responsible to reject the substance of the anti-homosexual verses and to conclude that, whether in a Jewish, Christian, or Muslim context, such discrimination is a perversion of all that is good and proper in ethical monotheism. In this regard, consider the statement of Rabbi Hillel, who said: "That which is hurtful to you, do not do to your neighbor."

Again, proscriptions of Leviticus 18:6-21 are a reflection of a disapproval of the incestuous sexual lifestyle of Akhenaten/Moses. The additional two sentences pertaining to homosexuality are, I believe, a subsequent addition to the original text and are an anomaly. They certainly do not easily tie into an analysis of the ethical monotheism created by Moses/Akhenaten.

APPENDIX TWO:

IDENTIFYING THE NAME OF GOD

In Chapter Six, I discussed a mountainous peak called Sarabit as being a semi-permanent place of residency to Moses/Akhenaten, his Levite companions and other compatriots. The group apparently lived in that area for some, or much, of the twenty-five years of the personal exile of Moses/Akhenaten. During that period, he and his companions developed the fabric and practices of the evolving monotheistic religion which became known as Judaism. One of their major disputes related to establishing the name of "God"; they had to reach a resolution. Readers familiar with Hebrew are aware that, as Osman reflects in his writings, the solution was to write the primary Hebrew name of God, as YHWH, and to verbalize that name as Adonai (being a theonym for God).

We will now review Exodus 3 and 4, and paraphrase the text to correlate the Hebrew and the English translations with the subjects of identifying the name of God (and the compromise reached in using the theonym, Adonai) and of establishing the new religion. As noted in Chapter Seven, these two Torah chapters set forth, in Hebrew, five forms of the word for God, two combinations of those forms and a strange juxtaposition of those names in Exodus 4:10. Those words for God are highlighted in bold type. Note that my paraphrasing on these subjects is set forth on the next several pages in the column marked "Rewrite."

Vs.	Hebrew	Traditional Translation	Rewrite
3:1	וּמֹשֶׁה הָיָה רֹעֶה אֶת־צֹאן יִתְרוֹ חֹתְנוֹ כֹּהֵן מִדְיָן וַיִּנְהַג אֶת־הַצֹּאן אַחַר הַמִּדְבָּר וַיָּבֹא אֶל־הַר הָאֱלֹהִים חֹרֵבָה׃	Now Moses was keeping the flock of Jethro, his father-in-law, the priest of Midian; and he led the flock to the farthest end of the wilderness, and came to the mountain of God, to Horeb.	Moses came to the mountain of Sarabit and lived there.
3:6	וַיֹּאמֶר אָנֹכִי אֱלֹהֵי אָבִיךָ אֱלֹהֵי אַבְרָהָם אֱלֹהֵי יִצְחָק וֵאלֹהֵי יַעֲקֹב וַיַּסְתֵּר מֹשֶׁה פָּנָיו כִּי יָרֵא מֵהַבִּיט אֶל־הָאֱלֹהִים׃	Moreover He said: "I am the God of thy father, the God of Abraham, the God of Isaac, and the God of Jacob." And Moses hid his face; for he was afraid to look upon God.	God said to Moses: "I am the God of your father [singular], the God of Abraham, Isaac and Jacob."
3:7	וַיֹּאמֶר יְהוָה רָאֹה רָאִיתִי אֶת־עֳנִי עַמִּי אֲשֶׁר בְּמִצְרָיִם וְאֶת־צַעֲקָתָם שָׁמַעְתִּי מִפְּנֵי נֹגְשָׂיו כִּי יָדַעְתִּי אֶת־מַכְאֹבָיו׃	And the LORD said: "I have surely seen the affliction of My people that are in Egypt, and have heard their cry by reason of their taskmasters; for I know their pains;"	During the period of residence in Sarabit, the Hebrews of Goshen were opprssed by the then reigning pharoah.
3:9	וְעַתָּה הִנֵּה צַעֲקַת בְּנֵי־יִשְׂרָאֵל בָּאָה אֵלָי וְגַם־רָאִיתִי אֶת־הַלַּחַץ אֲשֶׁר מִצְרַיִם לֹחֲצִים אֹתָם׃	"And now, behold, the cry of the children of Israel has come to Me; moreover I have seen the oppression wherewith the Egyptians oppress them."	The children of Goshen were beset by the Pharoah of Oppression. [We will expand on this rewrite below.]
3:10	וְעַתָּה לְכָה וְאֶשְׁלָחֲךָ אֶל־פַּרְעֹה וְהוֹצֵא אֶת־עַמִּי בְנֵי־יִשְׂרָאֵל מִמִּצְרָיִם׃	"Come now therefore, and I will send you to Pharaoh, that you may bring forth My people the children of Israel out of Egypt."	God said that Moses must bring forth the children of Goshen (Hebrews) from Egypt. "Moses, you need new people to form a base for your religion."

Vs.	Hebrew	Traditional Translation	Rewrite
3:11	וַיֹּאמֶר מֹשֶׁה אֶל־הָאֱלֹהִים מִי אָנֹכִי כִּי אֵלֵךְ אֶל־פַּרְעֹה וְכִי אוֹצִיא אֶת־בְּנֵי יִשְׂרָאֵל מִמִּצְרָיִם׃	And Moses said to God: "Who am I, that I should go to Pharaoh, and that I should bring forth the children of Israel out of Egypt?"	Moses resisted the call to return to Egypt to seek to either recover the throne, or, alternatively, to obtain the release of the Hebrews of Goshen. He questioned: "Who am I that I should go to the pharoah and I should bring forth the children of Goshen out of Egypt?"
3:12	וַיֹּאמֶר כִּי־אֶהְיֶה עִמָּךְ וְזֶה־לְּךָ הָאוֹת כִּי אָנֹכִי שְׁלַחְתִּיךָ בְּהוֹצִיאֲךָ אֶת־הָעָם מִמִּצְרַיִם תַּעַבְדוּן אֶת־הָאֱלֹהִים עַל הָהָר הַזֶּה׃	And He said: "Certainly I will be with you; and this shall be the token to you, that I have sent you: when you have brought forth the people out of Egypt, you shall serve God upon this mountain."	God reassured Moses/Akhenaten and said that, when the Exodus will occur, all of the émigrés should return to Sarabit and other high places to carry on the movement.
3:13	וַיֹּאמֶר מֹשֶׁה אֶל־הָאֱלֹהִים הִנֵּה אָנֹכִי בָא אֶל־בְּנֵי יִשְׂרָאֵל וְאָמַרְתִּי לָהֶם אֱלֹהֵי אֲבוֹתֵיכֶם שְׁלָחַנִי אֲלֵיכֶם וְאָמְרוּ־לִי מַה־שְּׁמוֹ מָה אֹמַר אֲלֵהֶם׃	And Moses said to God: "Behold, when I come to the children of Israel, and shall say to them: The God of your fathers has sent me to you; and they shall say to me: What is His name? what shall I say to them?"	Moses questioned God: "What do I call you when I approach the Hebrews in Goshen? They call you YHWH; I call you Aten."
3:14	וַיֹּאמֶר אֱלֹהִים אֶל־מֹשֶׁה אֶהְיֶה אֲשֶׁר אֶהְיֶה וַיֹּאמֶר כֹּה תֹאמַר לִבְנֵי יִשְׂרָאֵל אֶהְיֶה שְׁלָחַנִי אֲלֵיכֶם׃	And God said to Moses: "I AM THAT I AM"; and He said: "Thus shall you say to the children of Israel: I AM has sent me to you."	God answers: "What's in a name? What is important is that I exist (I AM THAT I AM). But if you insist, make everyone happy! Write my name as YHWH, but pronounce my name as Adonai [being my Adon, in Hebrew; my Aten, in Egyptian]."

Vs.	Hebrew	Traditional Translation	Rewrite
3:15	וַיֹּאמֶר עוֹד אֱלֹהִים אֶל־מֹשֶׁה כֹּה־תֹאמַר אֶל־בְּנֵי יִשְׂרָאֵל יְהוָה אֱלֹהֵי אֲבֹתֵיכֶם אֱלֹהֵי אַבְרָהָם אֱלֹהֵי יִצְחָק וֵאלֹהֵי יַעֲקֹב שְׁלָחַנִי אֲלֵיכֶם זֶה־שְּׁמִי לְעֹלָם וְזֶה זִכְרִי לְדֹר דֹּר׃	And God said moreover to Moses: 'Thus shall you say to the children of Israel: The LORD, the God of your fathers, the God of Abraham, the God of Isaac, and the God of Jacob, has sent me to you; this is My name for ever, and this is My memorial to all generations."	God further said that you shall tell the children of Goshen (Hebrews): "The Lord, the God of your fathers, the God of Abraham, of Isaac and Jacob, sent me to you." [We will expand upon this rewrite, and the comparison to verse 3:6, below.]
3:16	לֵךְ וְאָסַפְתָּ אֶת־זִקְנֵי יִשְׂרָאֵל וְאָמַרְתָּ אֲלֵהֶם יְהוָה אֱלֹהֵי אֲבֹתֵיכֶם נִרְאָה אֵלַי אֱלֹהֵי אַבְרָהָם יִצְחָק וְיַעֲקֹב לֵאמֹר פָּקֹד פָּקַדְתִּי אֶתְכֶם וְאֶת־הֶעָשׂוּי לָכֶם בְּמִצְרָיִם׃	"Go, and gather the elders of Israel together, and say to them: 'The LORD, the God of your fathers, the God of Abraham, of Isaac, and of Jacob, has appeared to me, saying: "I have surely remembered you, and seen that which is done to you in Egypt.""	God directed Moses to go and tell his chiefs at Sarabit that they must return to Egypt.
3:18	וְשָׁמְעוּ לְקֹלֶךָ וּבָאתָ אַתָּה וְזִקְנֵי יִשְׂרָאֵל אֶל־מֶלֶךְ מִצְרַיִם וַאֲמַרְתֶּם אֵלָיו יְהוָה אֱלֹהֵי הָעִבְרִיִּים נִקְרָה עָלֵינוּ וְעַתָּה נֵלְכָה־נָּא דֶּרֶךְ שְׁלֹשֶׁת יָמִים בַּמִּדְבָּר וְנִזְבְּחָה לַיהוָה אֱלֹהֵינוּ׃	"And they shall hearken to your voice. And you shall come, you and the elders of Israel, to the king of Egypt, and you shall say to him: 'The LORD, the God of the Hebrews, has met with us. And now let us go, we pray you, three days' journey into the wilderness, that we may sacrifice to the LORD our God.'"	God stated that Moses/Akhenaten should: "Tell your supporters that you are going to confront the new Pharaoh of Egypt."
4:1	וַיַּעַן מֹשֶׁה וַיֹּאמֶר וְהֵן לֹא־יַאֲמִינוּ לִי וְלֹא יִשְׁמְעוּ בְּקֹלִי כִּי יֹאמְרוּ לֹא־נִרְאָה אֵלֶיךָ יְהוָה׃	And Moses answered and said: "But, behold, they will not believe me, nor hearken to my voice; for they will say: 'The LORD has not appeared to you.'"	Moses again questioned God and said: "The Egyptian priests and the Hebrews of Goshen will not believe me."

Vs.	Hebrew	Traditional Translation	Rewrite
4:2	[ב חֶזֶה] הוָה אֵלָיו יְהֹוָה וַיֹּאמֶר מַזֶּה [מַה־זֶּה] בְיָדֶךָ וַיֹּאמֶר מַטֶּה (מָה־זֶּה בְיָדֶךָ):	And the LORD said to him: "What is that in your hand?" And he said: "A rod."	(4:2 through 4:8) God responded: Show the Egyptian priests the secret signs of the sed festival to prove your legitimacy and primacy.
4:3	וַיֹּאמֶר הַשְׁלִיכֵהוּ אַרְצָה וַיַּשְׁלִכֵהוּ אַרְצָה וַיְהִי לְנָחָשׁ וַיָּנָס מֹשֶׁה מִפָּנָיו:	And He said: "Cast it on the ground." And he cast it on the ground, and it became a serpent; and Moses fled from before it.	
4:4	וַיֹּאמֶר יְהֹוָה אֶל־מֹשֶׁה שְׁלַח יָדְךָ וֶאֱחֹז בִּזְנָבוֹ וַיִּשְׁלַח יָדוֹ וַיַּחֲזֶק בּוֹ וַיְהִי לְמַטֶּה בְּכַפּוֹ:	And the LORD said to Moses: "Put forth your hand, and take it by the tail," and he put forth his hand, and laid hold of it, and it became a rod in his hand,	
4:5	לְמַעַן יַאֲמִינוּ כִּי־נִרְאָה אֵלֶיךָ יְהֹוָה אֱלֹהֵי אֲבֹתָם אֱלֹהֵי אַבְרָהָם אֱלֹהֵי יִצְחָק וֵאלֹהֵי יַעֲקֹב:	"that they may believe that the LORD, the God of their fathers, the God of Abraham, the God of Isaac, and the God of Jacob, has appeared to you."	
4:6	וַיֹּאמֶר יְהֹוָה לוֹ עוֹד הָבֵא־נָא יָדְךָ בְּחֵיקֶךָ וַיָּבֵא יָדוֹ בְּחֵיקוֹ וַיּוֹצִאָהּ וְהִנֵּה יָדוֹ מְצֹרַעַת כַּשָּׁלֶג:	And the LORD said furthermore to him: "Put now your hand into your bosom." And he put his hand into his bosom; and when he took it out, behold, his hand was leprous, as white as snow.	
4:7	וַיֹּאמֶר הָשֵׁב יָדְךָ אֶל־חֵיקֶךָ וַיָּשֶׁב יָדוֹ אֶל־חֵיקוֹ וַיּוֹצִאָהּ מֵחֵיקוֹ וְהִנֵּה־שָׁבָה כִּבְשָׂרוֹ:	And He said: "Put your hand back into your bosom." And he put his hand back into his bosom; and when he took it out of his bosom, behold, it was turned again as his other flesh.	
4:8	וְהָיָה אִם־לֹא יַאֲמִינוּ לָךְ וְלֹא יִשְׁמְעוּ לְקֹל הָאֹת הָרִאשׁוֹן וְהֶאֱמִינוּ לְקֹל הָאֹת הָאַחֲרוֹן:	"And it shall come to pass, if they will not believe you, neither hearken to the voice of the first sign, that they will believe the voice of the latter sign."	

Vs.	Hebrew	Traditional Translation	Rewrite
4:9	וְהָיָה אִם־לֹא יַאֲמִינוּ גַּם לִשְׁנֵי הָאֹתוֹת הָאֵלֶּה וְלֹא יִשְׁמְעוּן לְקֹלֶךָ וְלָקַחְתָּ מִמֵּימֵי הַיְאֹר וְשָׁפַכְתָּ הַיַּבָּשָׁה וְהָיוּ הַמַּיִם אֲשֶׁר תִּקַּח מִן־הַיְאֹר וְהָיוּ לְדָם בַּיַּבָּשֶׁת׃	"And it shall come to pass, if they will not believe even these two signs, neither hearken to your voice, that you shall take of the water of the river, and pour it upon the dry land; and the water which you take out of the river shall become blood upon the dry land."	God said that the priests will believe at least one of the sed signs.
4:10	וַיֹּאמֶר מֹשֶׁה אֶל־יְהוָה בִּי אֲדֹנָי לֹא אִישׁ דְּבָרִים אָנֹכִי גַּם מִתְּמוֹל גַּם מִשִּׁלְשֹׁם גַּם מֵאָז דַּבֶּרְךָ אֶל־עַבְדֶּךָ כִּי כְבַד־פֶּה וּכְבַד לָשׁוֹן אָנֹכִי׃	And Moses said to the LORD: "Oh Lord, I am not a man of words, neither heretofore, nor since You have spoken to Your servant; for I am slow of speech, and of a slow tongue."	Moses/Akhenaten states, plaintively: "Please, my Aten, I don't speak Hebrew well and the children of Goshen will not understand me." [We will expand on this rewrite below].
4:12	וְעַתָּה לֵךְ וְאָנֹכִי אֶהְיֶה עִם־פִּיךָ וְהוֹרֵיתִיךָ אֲשֶׁר תְּדַבֵּר׃	Now therefore go, and I will be with your mouth, and teach you what you shall speak."	God answered, you can do it!
4:13	וַיֹּאמֶר בִּי אֲדֹנָי שְׁלַח־נָא בְּיַד־תִּשְׁלָח׃	And he said: 'Oh Lord, send, I pray You, by the hand of him whom You will send.'	Moses pleaded: "Please, my Aten, send someone who will assist me with communicating what must be said to the Egyptians and also to the children of Goshen."
4:14	וַיִּחַר־אַף יְהוָה בְּמֹשֶׁה וַיֹּאמֶר הֲלֹא אַהֲרֹן אָחִיךָ הַלֵּוִי יָדַעְתִּי כִּי־דַבֵּר יְדַבֵּר הוּא וְגַם הִנֵּה־הוּא יֹצֵא לִקְרָאתֶךָ וְרָאֲךָ וְשָׂמַח בְּלִבּוֹ׃	And the anger of the LORD was kindled against Moses, and He said: "Is there not Aaron your brother the Levite? I know that he can speak well. And also, behold, he comes forth to meet you; and when he sees you, he will be glad in his heart."	God responded: "You have a brother [which is the first introduction of Aaron in the Torah] who can speak well. When he sees you he will be glad to help."

138

Vs.	Hebrew	Traditional Translation	Rewrite
4:17	וְאֶת־הַמַּטֶּה הַזֶּה תִּקַּח בְּיָדֶךָ אֲשֶׁר תַּעֲשֶׂה־בּוֹ אֶת־הָאֹתֹת׃	"And you shalt take in your hand this rod, wherewith you shall do the signs."	God continued: "Now take this imperial staff to show your royal status and go back to Egypt."
4:19	וַיֹּאמֶר יְהוָה אֶל־מֹשֶׁה בְּמִדְיָן לֵךְ שֻׁב מִצְרָיִם כִּי־מֵתוּ כָּל־הָאֲנָשִׁים הַמְבַקְשִׁים אֶת־נַפְשֶׁךָ׃	And the LORD said to Moses in Midian: "Go, return into Egypt; for all the men are dead that sought your life."	God finished: "You can go back to Egypt because everyone who wanted to kill you is dead. Horemheb is dead! You will confront the new Pharaoh, Ramses I."
4:30	וַיְדַבֵּר אַהֲרֹן אֵת כָּל־הַדְּבָרִים אֲשֶׁר־דִּבֶּר יְהוָה אֶל־מֹשֶׁה וַיַּעַשׂ הָאֹתֹת לְעֵינֵי הָעָם׃	And Aaron spoke all the words which the LORD had spoken to Moses, and did the signs in the sight of the people.	Aaron became the spokesman and showed the Egyptian priests and the Hebrews of Goshen [collectively "people"] the signs of the sed festival.
4:31	וַיַּאֲמֵן הָעָם וַיִּשְׁמְעוּ כִּי־פָקַד יְהוָה אֶת־בְּנֵי יִשְׂרָאֵל וְכִי רָאָה אֶת־עָנְיָם וַיִּקְּדוּ וַיִּשְׁתַּחֲווּ׃	And the people believed; and when they heard that the LORD had remembered the children of Israel, and that He had seen their affliction, then they bowed their heads and worshipped.	And the Egyptian priests and the Hebrews of Goshen [collectively "the people"] were convinced and they bowed their heads and acknowledged the primacy of Akhenaten/Moses. [We will expand upon this rewrite below.]

The following are my extended comments pertaining to the above verses:

3:9

The children of Goshen were beset by the Pharaoh of Oppression. The Pharaoh of Oppression died. The successor pharaoh, Ramses I, apparently then invaded the space of Moses/Akhenaten and built a stela in the sacred space of Sarabit. Moses/Akhenaten, the Levites and the military entourage were shocked by the realization that they were under attack by Ramses I and they were further shocked by the realization that they needed new and additional followers to carry on the religious movement, in order for their group to survive. They needed "new blood."

3:15

God further said that you shall tell the children of Goshen (being the Hebrews): "The Lord, the God of your *fathers* [plural], the God of Abraham, Isaac and Jacob, sent me to you." As to this wording, when I was first learning liturgy, I understood the identification of Abraham, Isaac and Jacob to be an appositional phrase to the words "your fathers." This is probably a correct interpretation at this time. However, these words reflect a parallelism worth examining. This phraseology is parallel, but in contrast, to the expression of God to Moses/Akhenaten in Exodus 3:6, where God said to Moses: "I am the God of thy *father* [singular], the God of Abraham, Isaac and Jacob." This identification of the singular word "father," can only be translated and understood as being the specific father of Moses/Akhenaten. His biological father was Amenhotep III. In this sentence, the Hebrew forefathers Abraham, Isaac and Jacob could not have been an appositional phrase to the singular word "father." Therefore, the text in verse 3:6 suggests that God is the God of all *mankind*, whether Jewish or non-Jewish, and, specifically as to Moses/Akhenaten, the God of *his* father, Amenhotep III. This is noteworthy because, in this context, Amenhotep III had an incipient relationship to monotheism because of his exposure to his wife, Queen Tiye, and her relatives in Goshen, all of which is evidenced by the name of his royal barge, "*Aten* Gleams." It was therefore appropriate to specifically include his father in the text.

4:10

Moses/Akhenaten states, plaintively: "Please, my Aten, I don't speak Hebrew well and the children of Goshen will not understand me." This verse is key, because in this verse and in 4:13, Moses/Akhenaten still voiced his reluctance or fear to return to Egypt. He still referred to the monotheistic God as *his* Aten. If the reader reads Hebrew, the reader will see the strange juxtaposition of the words of verse

10. They are: "And Moses said unto the *LORD* [YHWH]: 'Oh, *Lord* [Aten], I am not a man of words …'" (emphasis added). Even the English translation reflects the second usage of the word lord, meaning Aten, by capitalizing the letter "L" followed by lower case letters. That contrast of words and spelling shows a not-so-subtle subtext of reference directly to *Aten*. Otherwise, the verse would have been different. In this regard, we show the two variable forms of this verse:

unto the LORD [YHWH]

And Moses said: ^"Oh, Lord, I am not a man of words."

With the insertion of the phrase "unto the LORD," the above translation sets forth the words of the Torah directly. Without that insertion, the text still makes sense, but stresses the personal relationship of Moses/Akhenaten to God, with his plaintive call to Aten. As written, the only reason for writing the actual Hebrew *word Adonai* (or Adoni) without again substituting the theonym for God (i.e., YHWH) is that Moses/Akhenaten actually spoke the words, "Please, my Aten."

Further, usage of the Hebrew word *bee*, which should be translated as "Please" (rather than "Oh"), is interesting. The phrase "Bee, Adonai" (or "Bee, Adoni") is archaic. The archaic form of the Hebrew shows that the words were expressed at an early time when Moses/Akhenaten had not yet returned to Egypt to lead the Hebrews out of Goshen and, consequently, when he was likely to have continued to speak Egyptian as his primary language. After all, because all of his compatriots also spoke Egyptian, he had no need to think or speak in Hebrew. Further, he then admits "I don't speak (Hebrew) well." If he were speaking Egyptian, his usage of the words Bee Adonai (or Bee Adoni) would have reflected his actual meaning: "Please, my Aten." It is apparent that, when the scenario suggested by this text was reduced to writing, the scrivener adopted the actual words of Moses/Akhenaten, but then inserted, before the actual utterance, the theonym for YHWH, in the phrase "unto the LORD," to make the case to later generations that Moses/Akhenaten was speaking directly to his monotheistic God in, and as a, Hebrew and not as an Egyptian.

4:30 to 4:31

And the Egyptian priests and the Hebrews of Goshen [collectively "the people"] were convinced and they bowed their heads and acknowledged the primacy of Akhenaten/Moses. They understood that he was the sole surviving male member of the monarchy of the Eighteenth Dynasty and that he had come to regain the throne or, alternatively, had come to obtain the release of the Hebrews of Goshen from bondage. In fact, Moses/Akhenaten would lead the mixed multitude from Egypt and thereby provide new blood for the movement. In these two verses, the Hebrew word for "the people" (being "Am") was used so that the reader could interpret that word to mean: The Hebrews of Goshen, the Egyptian priests, or, as suggested by me in the above rewrite, both the Hebrews *and* the Egyptian priests.

The reader may not agree with my rewrite of the Torah verses; but, with very little change of, and in, the sequence of words and interpretations thereof, the re-write (and the actual history as reflected in the actual Torah text) fits almost exactly the historical record and analysis given in Chapters Six and Seven. The clues found in the Torah, and the archaeological evidence of the Amarna era, corroborate the identities and motivations of the people we have studied in this book, who en-gaged in a great and successful struggle to create the Jewish religion and its ethos.

NOTES

Chapter Two

1. Ahmed Osman, *Moses and Akhenaten: The Secret History of Egypt at the Time of the Exodus* (Rochester, VT: Bear & Company, 2002), 130.

2. H. H. Ben-Sasson and Abraham Malamat, *A History of the Jewish People* (Cambridge, MA: Harvard UP, 1976), 40-43.

3. Charles Pope, "The Gospel According to Egypt," in *Domain of Man* (2004), http://www.domainofman.com.

4. Ibid.

5. Ibid., "Surest Signs of Piety."

6. Osman, *Moses and Akhenaten*, 130-131.

7. Richard Elliott Friedman, *Who Wrote the Bible?* (Englewood Cliffs, NJ: Prentice Hall, 1987), 86.

Chapter Three

1. Ahmed Osman, *The Hebrew Pharaohs of Egypt: The Secret Lineage of the Patriarch Joseph*, bk. 1 (Rochester, VT: Bear & Company, 2003), 111.

2. Ibid., 14.

3. Gen. 45:8.

4. Gen. 41:45.

5. Osman, *Hebrew Pharaohs*, bk. 1, 112-114.

6. Ibid., bk. 2, 156-158.

7. Ibid., bk. 1, 126-127.

8. Friedman, *Who Wrote the Bible?*, 66.

9. Osman, *Hebrew Pharaohs*, bk. 1, 63.

10. Ibid., 120.

11. Joseph H. Hertz, *The Pentateuch and Haftorahs: Hebrew Text, English translation and commentary* (London: Soncino Press, 1960), 189.

12. Osman, *Hebrew Pharaohs*, bk. 1, 71.

13. Osman *Hebrew Pharoahs*, bk. 1, 12.

14. Gen. 46:15–25; 46:27; Ex. 1:5.

15. Osman, *Hebrew Pharaohs*, bk. 1, 123.

16. H. Polano, *Selections from the Talmud*, trans. Michael Rodkinson (U.S.: Pacific Publishing Studio, 2011), 74.

Chapter Four

1. Osman, *Moses and Akhenaten*, 61-62.

2. Osman, *Hebrew Pharaohs*, bk. 1, 85-86.

3. Friedman, *Who Wrote the Bible?*, 82.

4. Osman, *Moses and Akhenaten*, 66.

5. Ahmed Osman, "Out of Egypt, Article # 10: Moses and Akhenaten – One and the Same Person," *Dwij.org*, 2002, http://dwij.org/forum/amarna/10_moses_akhenaten.htm.

6. Osman, *Moses and Akhenaten*, 66-67.

7. Pope, *Domain of Man*, "Surest Sign of Piety."

8. Hertz, *Pentateuch and Haftorahs*, 490.

9. Anneke Bart, "Anen," *Euler.slu.edu* (September 2008), http://euler.slu.edu/~bart/egyptianhtml/kings and Queens/Anen.html.

10. Osman, *Moses and Akhenaten*, 183.

11. Palano, *Selections from the Talmud*, 84.

12. Osman, *Moses and Akhenaten*, 32.

13. Shemuel and Zeev Safrai, *Haggadah of the Sages* (Jerusalem: Carta, 2009), 126.

14. Hertz, *Pentateuch and Haftorahs*, 660.

Chapter Five

1. Osman, *Moses and Akhenaten*, 181-182.

2. Ibid.

3. Pope, *Domain of Man*, "Surest Sign of Piety."

Chapter Six

1. Martin Berkowitz, *Haggadah for the American family: English service with directions* (Miami: Sacred Press, 1966).
2. Osman, *Moses and Akhenaten*, 62-63.
3. Ibid., 105.
4. Polano, *Selections from the Talmud*, 76-77.
5. Ex. 6:30; 7:1-2.
6. Osman, *Moses and Akhenaten*, 169.
7. See also Gen. 15:14; Ex. 3:21-22.
8. Ralph Ellis, *Scota, Egyptian Queen of Scots* (Cheshire: EDFU, 2006).
9 Shalom Goldman, liner notes to *Akhnaten*, Philip Glass, CBS Records Masterworks M2K 42457, CD, 1987.
10. Morris Silver, "Ancient Economics II: Topic A: Making a Case for a Technological Interpretation of the Parting of the Sea in Exodus," (Last modified 1998), http://www.angelfire.com/ms/ancecon/.
11. Polano, *Selections from the Talmud*, 89.
12. Steven M. Collins, "The Missing Simeonites," *Stevenmcollins.com* (2006), http://stevenmcollins.com/html/simeon.html.

Chapter Seven

1. Alfred J.Kolatch, *The Second Jewish Book of Why* (Middle Village, NY: Jonathan David Publishers, 2007), 208-210.
2. Ibid., 216.
3. Osman, *Moses and Akhenaten*, 175-178.
4. Ibid., 173.
5. Louis Finkelstein, introduction to *Haggadah of Passover*, translated by Maurice Samuel (New York: Hebrew Pub. Co., 1942).
6. Osman, *Moses and Akhenaten*, 181, quoting Ray Winfield Smith and Donald B. Redford, *The Akhenaten Temple Project* (Warminster, England: Aris & Phillips, 1976).
7. Prov.31:10-31.
8. Friedman, *Who Wrote the Bible?*, 193-196.
9. Hertz, *Pentateuch and Haftorahs*, 490.
10. Osman, *Moses and Akhenaten*, 170.

11. Polano, *Selections from the Talmud*, 95-96.

12. Osman, *Moses and Akhenaten*, 23-24.

13. Tracy R. Rich, "Rabbis, Priests, and Other Religious Functionaries," *Jewfaq.org* (2011), http://www.jewfaq.org/rabbi.htm.

14. Hertz, *Pentateuch and Haftorahs*, 291.

15. See Ex 28:36-40; 29:6; Num 15:38-9; Deut 22:12.

16. Friedman, *Who Wrote the Bible?*, 177-181.

17. Clara Moskowitz "Bible Possibly Written Centuries Earlier, Text Suggests," *Livescience.com*, January 15, 2010, http://www.livescience.com/8008-bible-possibly-written-centuries-earlier-text-suggests.html.

18. Moustafa Gadalla, *Historical Deception: The Untold Story of Ancient Egypt* (Erie, PA: Bastet Pub., 1996), 194.

19. Osman, *Moses and Akhenaten*, 166-169.

20. Jonathan Sacks, *A Letter in the Scroll: Understanding our Jewish Identity and Exploring the Legacy of the World's Oldest Religion* (New York: Free Press, 2000), 93, 100, 226.

21. Hertz, *Pentateuch and Haftorahs*, 505.

Chapter Eight

1. Friedman, *Who Wrote the Bible?*, 190.

2. Osman, *Moses and Akhenaten*, 22-23.

3. Robin Cohn, "Miriam the Prophetess," from newsletter *Biblical Women Week by Week*, July 10, 2011, http://www.robincohn.net/images/Miriam_the_Prophetess.pdf, quoting Carol Meyers, *Exodus* (Cambridge: Cambridge UP, 2005).

4. Dewayne Bryant, "Ancient Fragments of Moses' Song of the Sea," *Apologetics Press*, 2010, http://espanol.apologeticspress.org/articles/240361.

Chapter Nine

1. Osman, *Moses and Akhenaten*, 186-188.

2. Friedman, *Who Wrote the Bible?*, 201.

Epilogue

1. Abba Solomon Eban, *My People: The Story of the Jews* (New York: Behrman House, 1968).

2. Jill and Leon Uris, *Jerusalem, Song of Songs* (Garden City, NY: Doubleday, 1981).

3. Z. Harry Gutstein and Nathan Goldberg, *Passover Haggadah = Hagadah shel Pesah* (New York: J. Biegeleisen Co., 1963), p.10. See also p. 23-24.

Appendix II

1. Osman, *Moses and Akhenaten*, 51-52.
2. Ibid., 52-53.

Appendix V

1. Osman, *Hebrew Pharaohs*, bk. 1, 21-24.
2. Ibid., 24.
3. Ibid., 30.
4. Ibid., 49.

Appendix VI

1. Hertz, *Pentateuch and Haftorahs*, 201.

Appendix VII

1. Friedman, *Who Wrote the Bible?*, 101-102.

INDEX

Sheldon L. Lebold is a lifelong resident of the Chicagoland area. He graduated from the University of Chicago with a Bachelor of Arts Degree and from the University of Chicago Law School as a JD in 1960.

He is a practicing attorney, specializing in transactional law. He is highly involved with Jewish religious heritage. He has sung in synagogue choirs and is currently both a Baal Koray (Torah reader) and Baal Tekia (shofar blower). He and his wife, Ronda, were honored with the State of Israel Bonds Achievement Award (being Persons of the Year). Other accomplishments include actively pursuing the incorporation of a local community which later became a village. His secular interests include being a classical music aficionado and a die-hard Chicago Cubs baseball fan.